W9-AYE-561

How to Swear

An illustrated guide

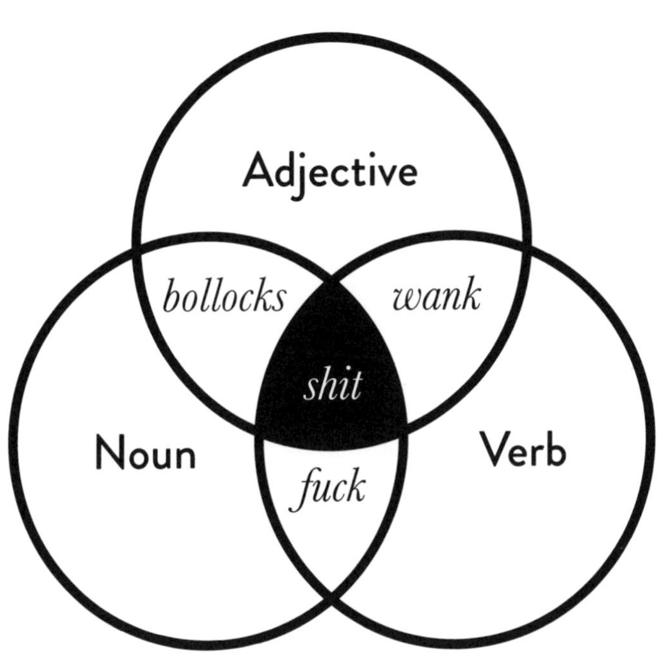

Stephen Wildish

3 5 7 9 10 8 6 4

Ebury Press, an imprint of Ebury Publishing
20 Vauxhall Bridge Road
London SW1V 2SA

Ebury Press is part of the Penguin Random House group of companies whose addresses can be found at global.penguinrandomhouse.com

First published by Ebury Press in 2017

www.penguin.co.uk

A CIP catalogue record for this book is available from the British Library

ISBN 9781785036415

Printed and bound in TBB, a. s. Slovakia

Dedicated to my fucking wife.

Contents

Introduction

Introduction

When executed correctly swearing can
be a true artform, a thing of beauty,
a way to diffuse pain or insult a colleague.
Perform it incorrectly and prepare
to make an arse of yourself.

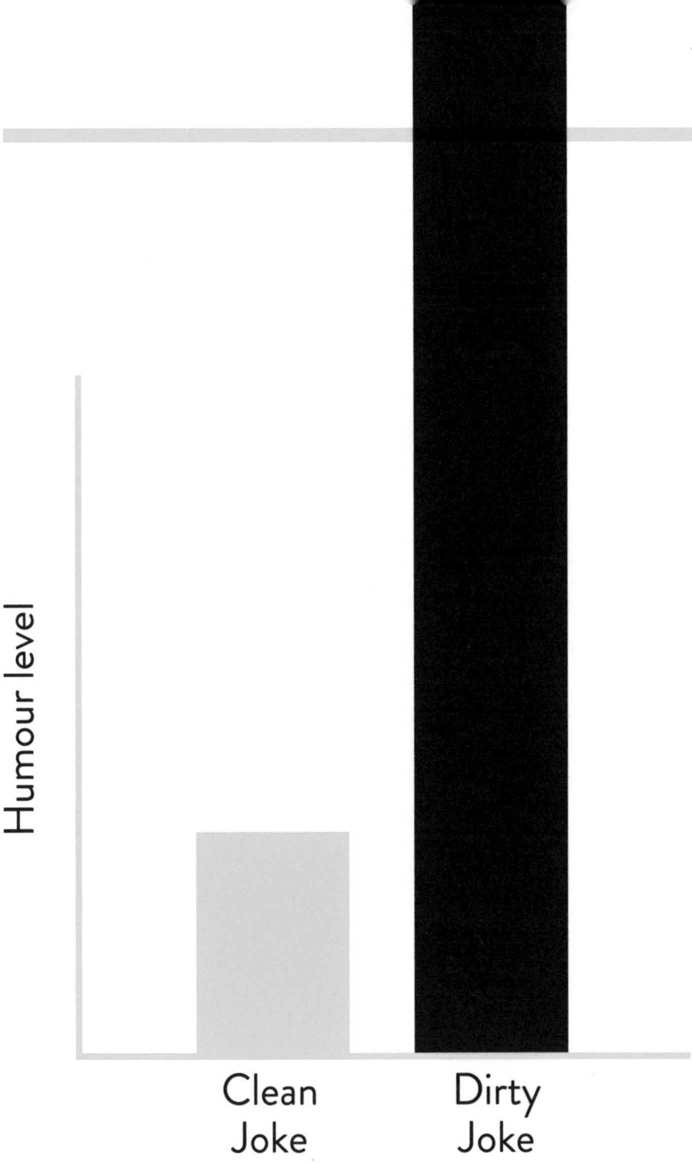

Humour level

Clean Joke

Dirty Joke

"UNDER CERTAIN CIRCUMSTANCES PROFANITY PROVIDES A RELIEF DENIED EVEN TO PRAYER"

Mark Twain

"OH FUCK, I SAID SHIT... OH SHIT I SAID FUCK!"

Queen Elizabeth

Devices for creative swearing

POETIC DEVICES

Metaphor

"You're a dickhead"

Simile

"You look like shit"

Alliteration

"Bloody bollocks"

Rhyme

"Fuck a duck"

EXCRETIONS

Using bodily excretions and organs

"A piece of shit"

"Piss off"

Devices for creative swearing

ACTIVITES

Suggest that the person engages in an unsavoury activity

"Go fuck yourself"

Incest

"Motherfucker"

Sodomy

"Bugger"

Fellatio

"Cocksucker"

Bestiality

"Sheepshagger"

Swear words ranked by severity

1. CUNT
2. FUCK
3. WANKER
4. SHIT
5. BOLLOCKS
6. ARSEHOLE
7. TWAT
8. DICKHEAD

9 BASTARD
10 ARSE
11 PISS
12 BUGGER
13 BALLS
14 CRAP
15 BLOODY
16 GOD

A brief history of blasphemy

The term profane is derived from the latin **profanus** meaning **outside of the temple**.

Offensive swear words change over time according to cultural attitudes towards God, sex and excretions.

For most of history, it has been considered highly offensive to utter God's name in vain or to mock the traditions of the church. It would have been very unusual to hear someone say 'oh God' or 'bloody hell'. Phrases that are now commonplace.

Although fairly respectable before, the main expletive of the eighteenth century was **bloody**. It was heavily tabooed during 1750–1920. **Bloody** was controversial until the 1960s, but the word has become a tame expletive or intensifier.

Current taboos are for sexual acts and excretions (words that were commonplace in past centuries).

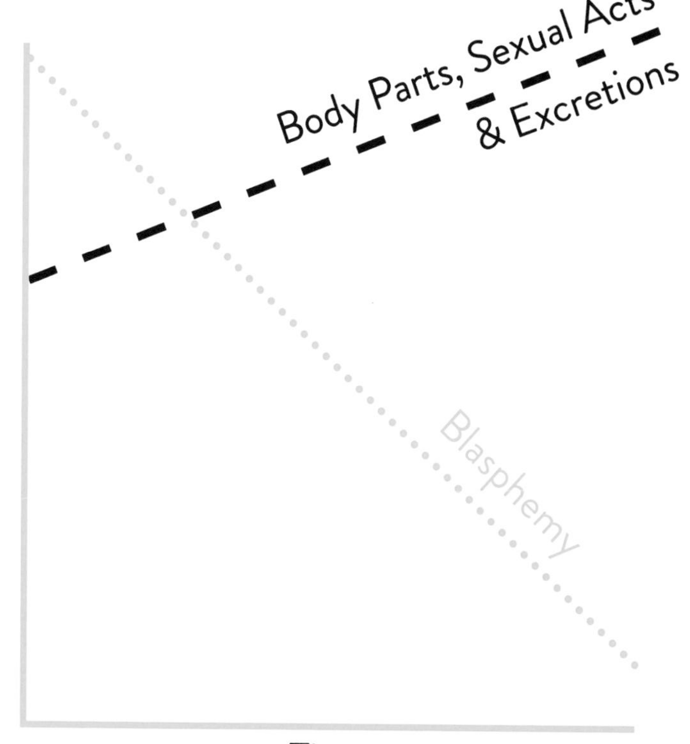
Body Parts, Sexual Acts
& Excretions
Blasphemy
Offensiveness
Time

Building an effective insult

By adding a rhythmic **fuck** and an additional adjective, you can build an effective insult from a baseword. On the example here we have the added bonus that you can expand the word **dick** into **dickhead**. Most body parts can be expanded in this way (e.g. **arse** expands to **arsehole**).

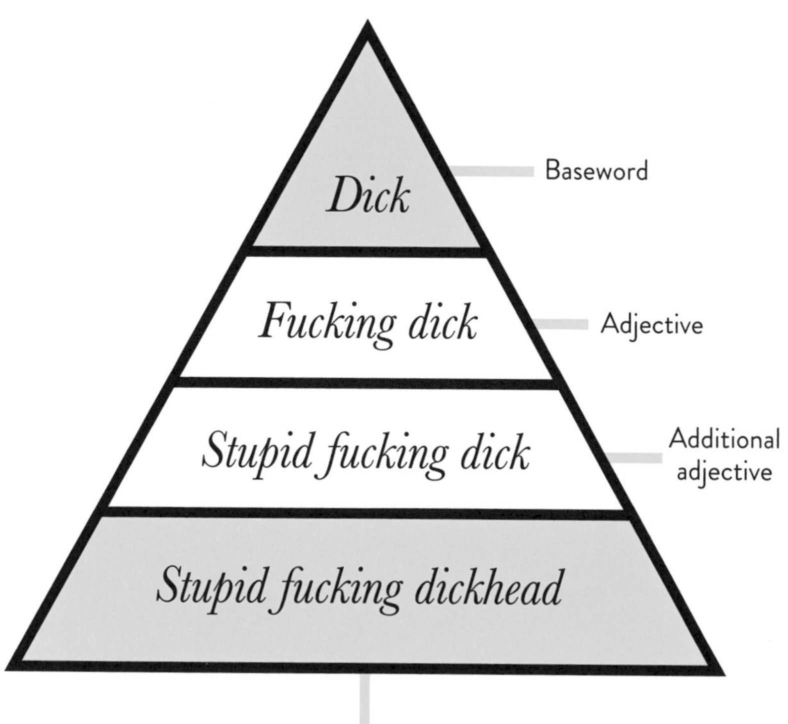

Expand on any remaining words (e.g. dick becomes dickhead)

Order of adjectives in insults

Adjectives in the English language follow this order:

OPINION

SIZE

AGE

SHAPE

COLOUR

ORIGIN

MATERIAL

PURPOSE

The same is true for insults...

Correct order

"You stupid, little, old, fat dickhead"

Incorrect order

"You old, fat, little, stupid dickhead"

Correct order

"You smelly old twat"

Incorrect order

"You old smelly twat"

Chapter 1

{*Fuck*}

Fuck

A word with origins in the act of sexual intercourse. One of the most versatile words in the English language, it can be used as a noun, a verb (both transitive and intransitive), an adjective, an interjection, imperative, conjunction or an adverb. It can also be used as an interjection and a grammatical ejaculation.

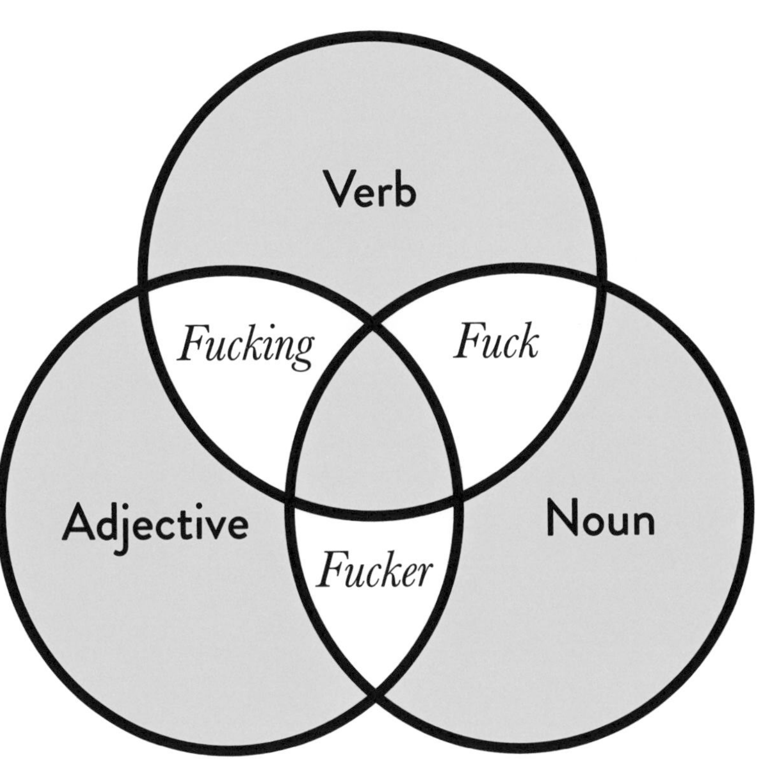
Verb
Fucking
Fuck
Adjective
Noun
Fucker

Etymology of Fuck

There are many theories about the history of the word fuck, some more convincing than others. Here are two of the most widely circulated:

German Roots

Fuck has similar roots in German words like **ficken** (to fuck) or the Dutch word **fokken** (to breed).

Greek Roots

The Greek word **phyō** has serveral meanings, including to beget or to give birth to.

Common Germanic

Fuk

English	Dutch	German
Fuck	*Fokken*	*Ficken*

You gave birth to a stupid fuck!

Fuck as an adjective, verb, noun and grammatical ejaculation

"Fucking fuck!

Grammatical ejaculation

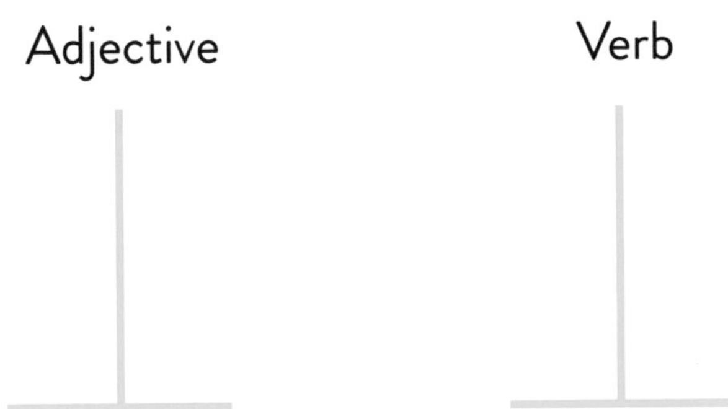

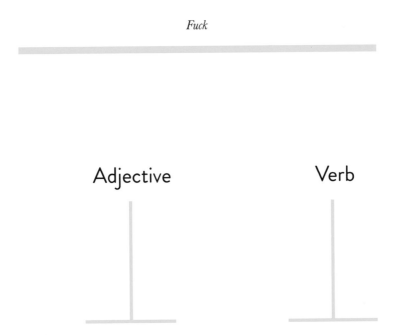

The fucking fucker's fucked"

Correct use of fucking as an infix

The correct use places the infix in the middle or the first half of the destination word.

Correct

"Abso-fucking-lutely"

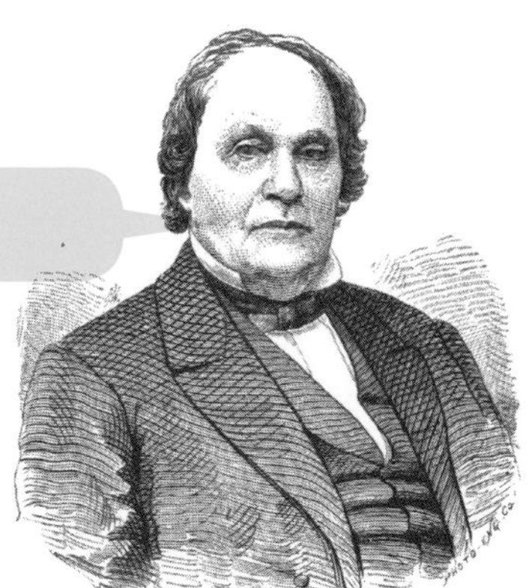

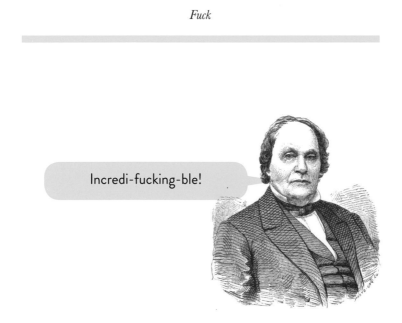

"Absolut-fucking-ly"

Incorrect

Correct use of fuck as an intensifier

The correct use places the intensifier toward the end of the phrase. Addition of the definite article can be required.

"None of your business"

"None of your fucking business"

“Shut the fuck up”

Conjugation of fuck

This is where the word fuck excels. Fuck can be placed before most pronouns, creating varying meanings.

Subject	Object	Number	Gender	Person
I	Fuck me	Singular	-	1st
You	Fuck you	Singular or Plural	-	2nd
He	Fuck him	Singular	Masculine	3rd
She	Fuck her	Singular	Feminine	3rd
It	Fuck it	Singular	-	3rd
This	Fuck this	Singular	-	3rd
They	Fuck them	Plural	-	3rd

Fuck...

you
her
him
them
it
this
that
all
off

Acceptability of fuck and fuck derivatives

It is not advisable to use the word fuck in front of vicars or children. Therefore, use one of the examples here. All can replace the word **fuck** or **fucking** (e.g. oh for fudge sake, flipping heck!). How far you go down the chart is for you to judge based on the occasion and the stuffiness of the guest you wish to 'feck off'.

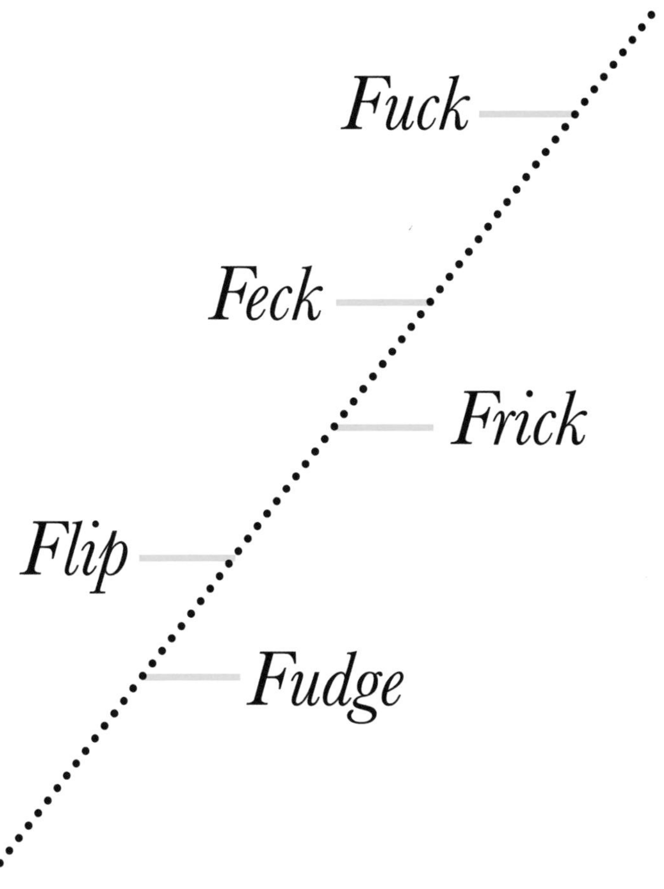
Fuck
Feck
Frick
Flip
Fudge
Offensiveness

Motherfucker as an adjective and noun

Noun

"Motherfucker, you fucked...

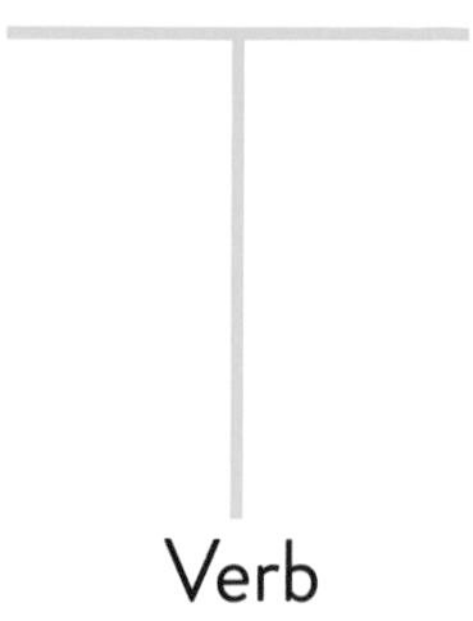

Verb

...my motherfucking mother"

Adjective

Fucking senses

Fucking tenses

Tense	Meaning	Example
Simple past	He did it	He fucked
Simple present	He usually does it	He fucks
Past progressive	He was doing it at that time	He was fucking
Present progressive	He is doing it now	He is fucking
Past perfect	Before that time, he had already	He had fucked
Present perfect	He has done it already	He has fucked
Future	He will do it	He will fuck

Passive

FUCK ME
FUCK IT
FUCK THIS

Aggressive

FUCK OFF
FUCK YOU

The F word

The power of fuck is such that it is often referred to as **the F word**. There are only a few words bestowed with this honor (or dishonour). The F word has also been used to ironically refer to feminism, as a pejorative homophobic slur, or, worst of all, a TV show about food.

THE F WORD

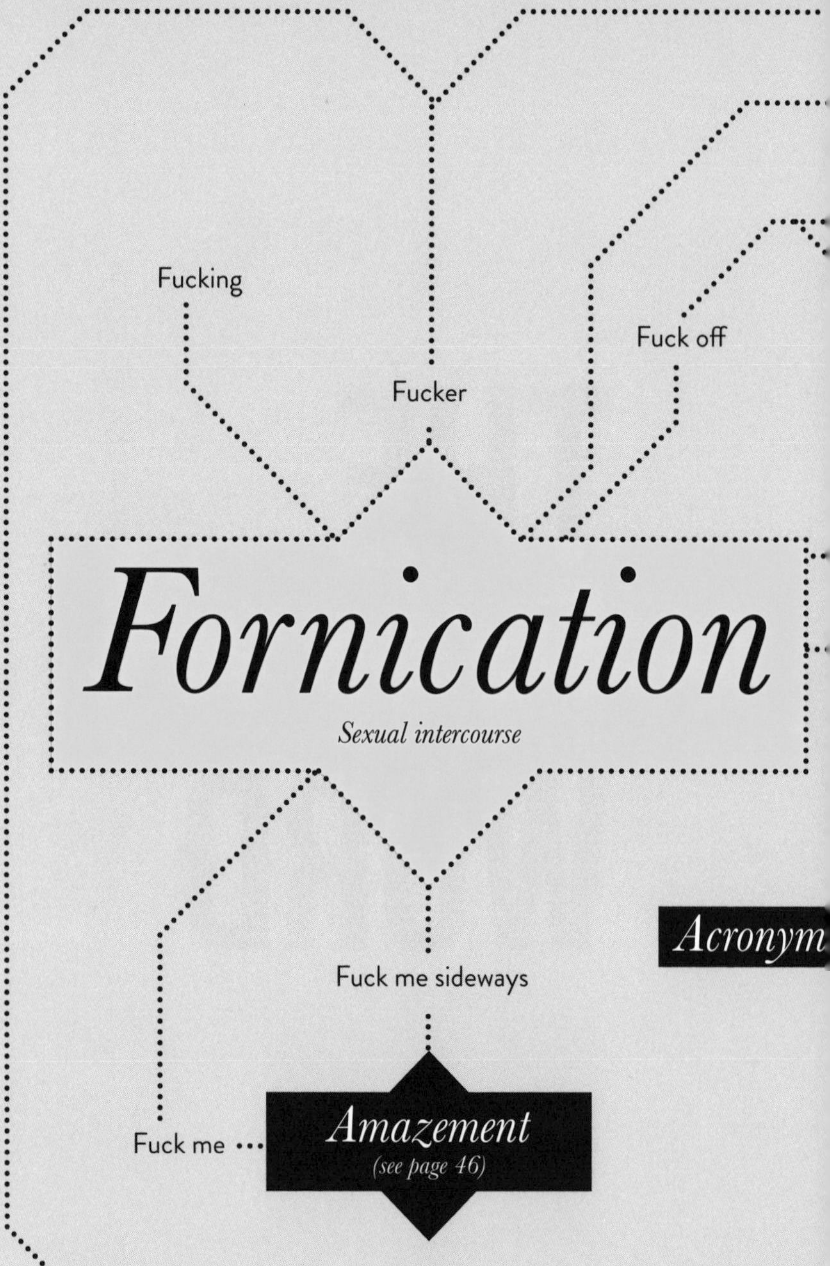

Fucking

Fuck off

Fucker

Fornication

Sexual intercourse

Acronym

Fuck me sideways

Fuck me

Amazement

(see page 46)

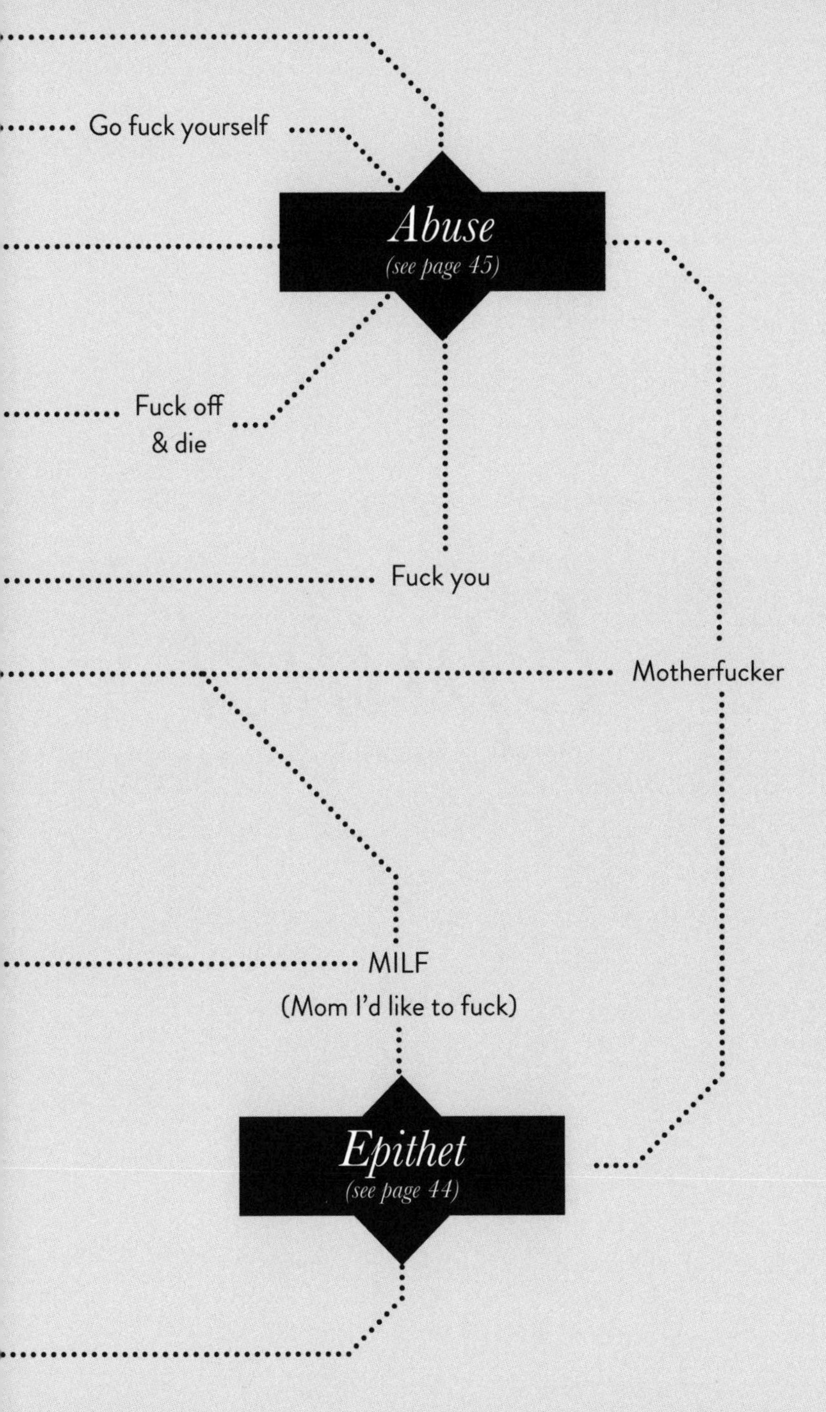
Go fuck yourself
Abuse
(see page 45)
Fuck off
& die
Fuck you
Motherfucker
MILF
(Mom I'd like to fuck)
Epithet
(see page 44)

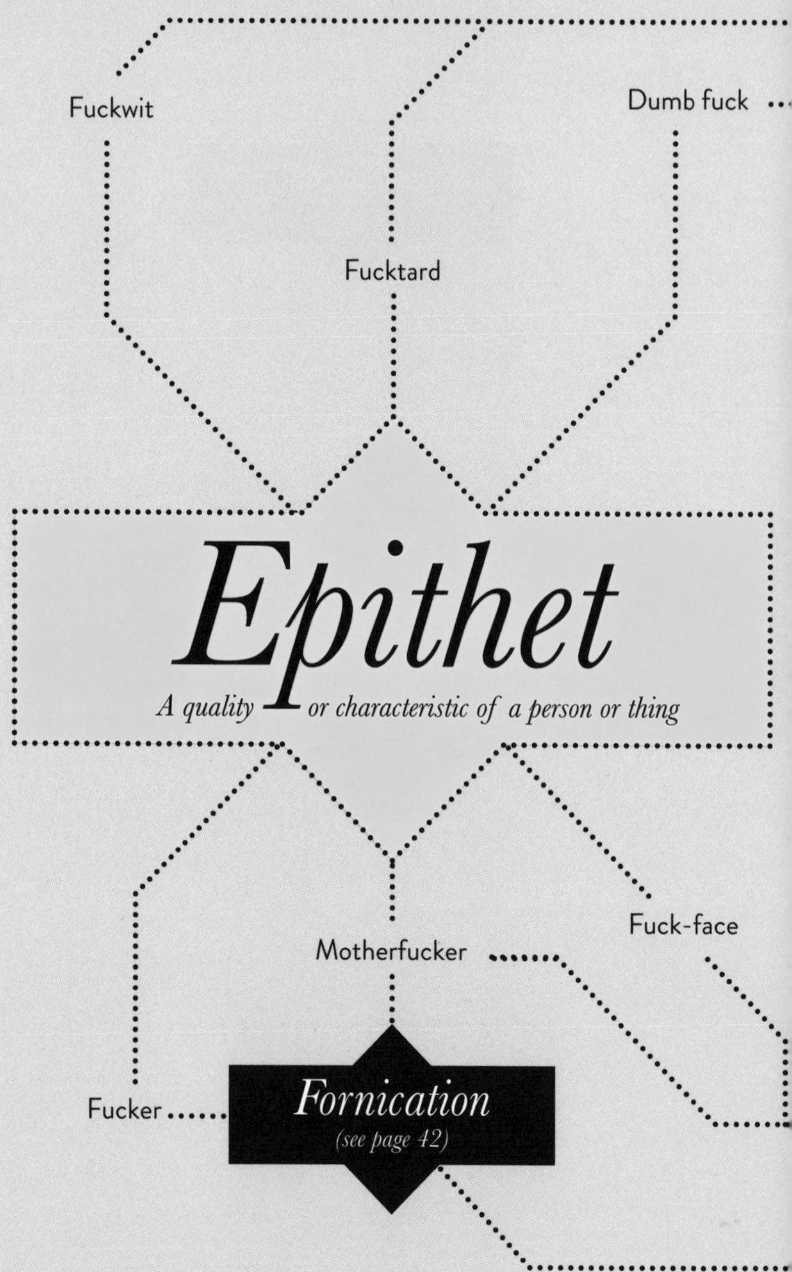
Fuckwit
Dumb fuck
Fucktard
Epithet
A quality or characteristic of a person or thing
Fuck-face
Motherfucker
Fucker
Fornication
(see page 42)

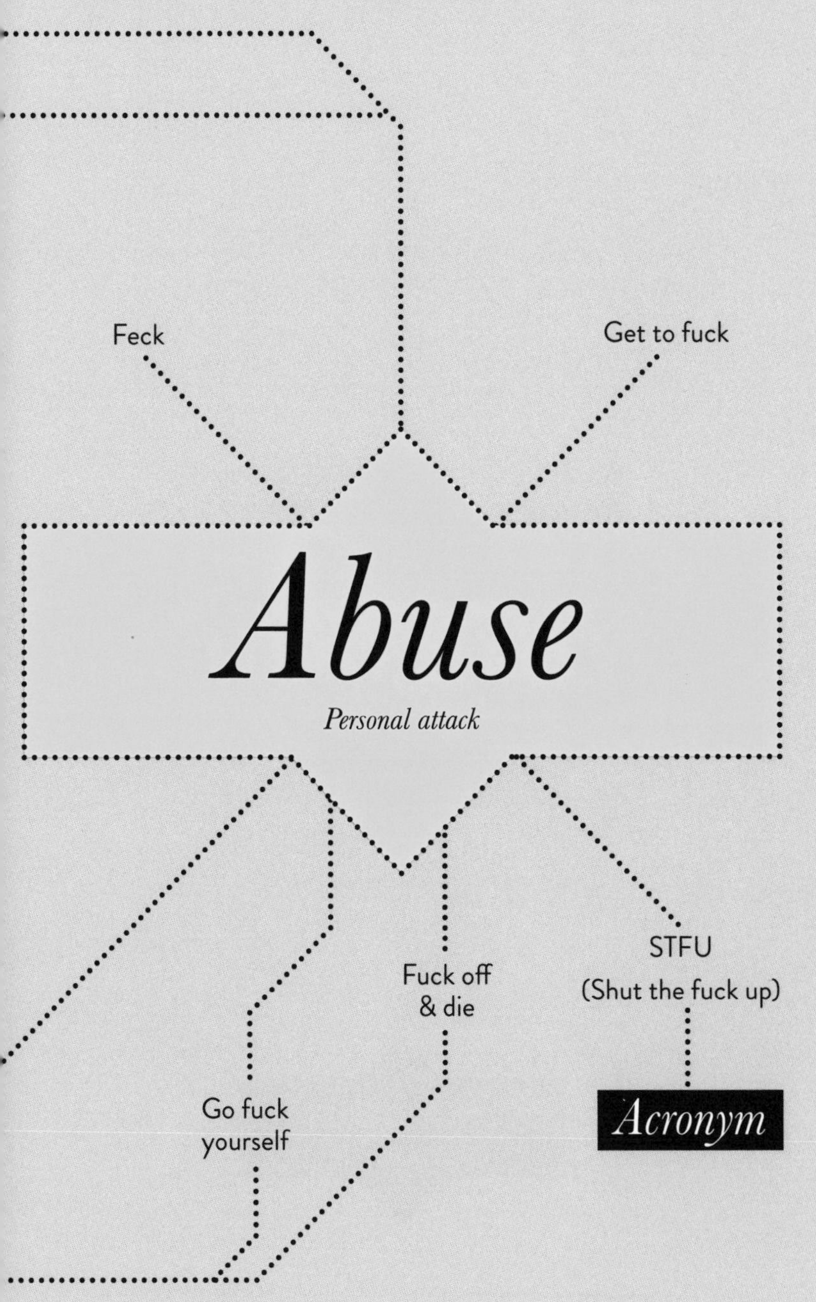
Feck
Get to fuck
Abuse
Personal attack
STFU
(Shut the fuck up)
Fuck off
& die
Go fuck
yourself
Acronym

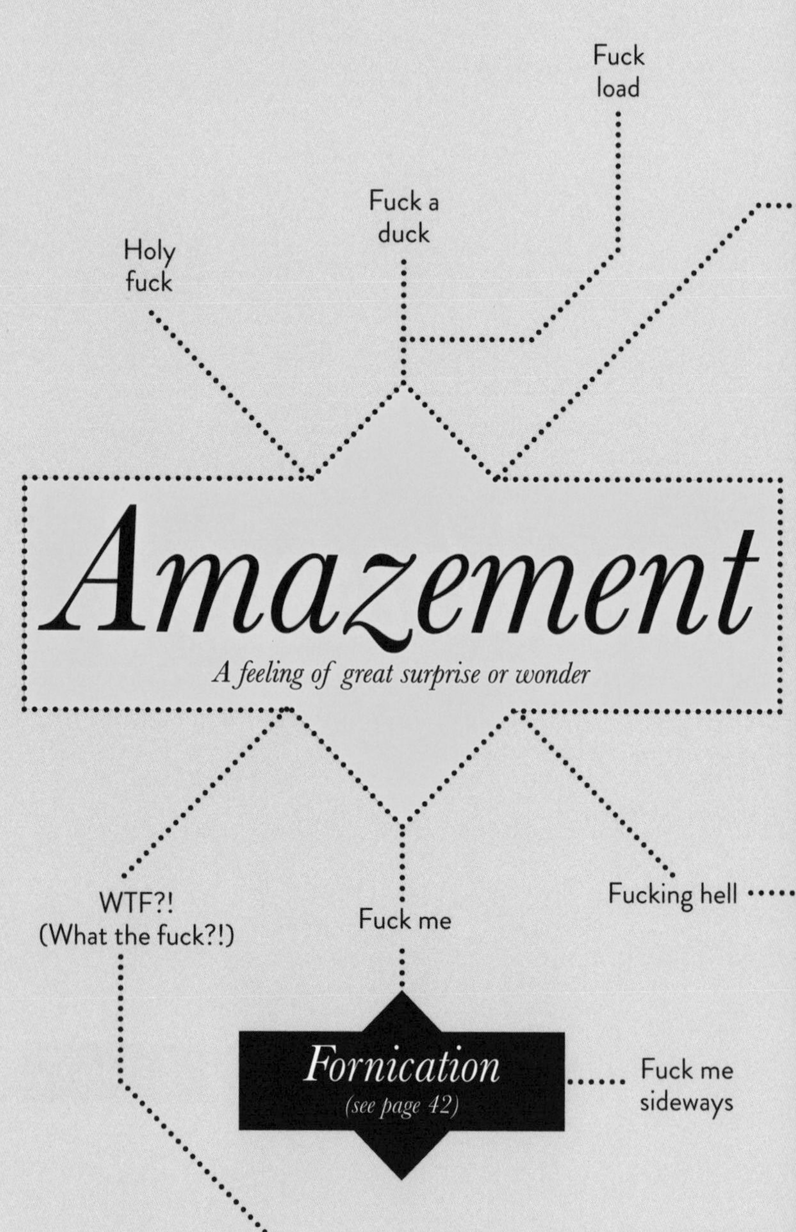
Fuck
load
Fuck a
duck
Holy
fuck
Amazement
A feeling of great surprise or wonder
WTF?!
(What the fuck?!)
Fuck me
Fucking hell
Fornication
(see page 42)
Fuck me
sideways

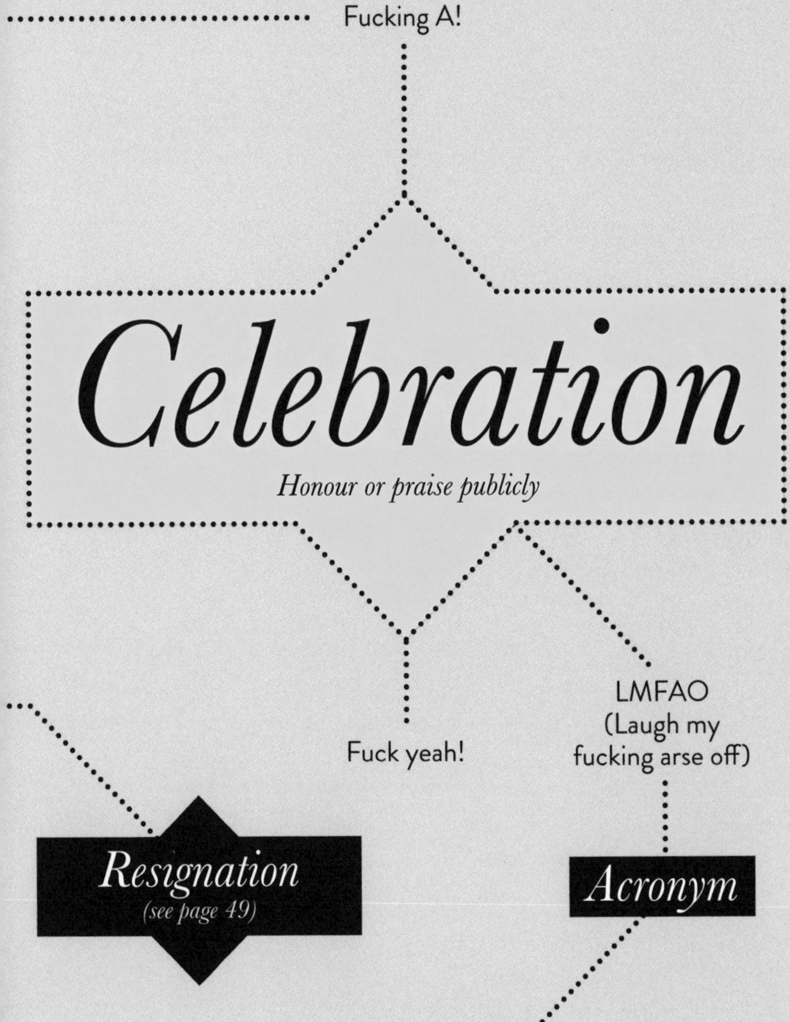

Fucking A!

Celebration

Honour or praise publicly

Fuck yeah!

LMFAO
(Laugh my
fucking arse off)

Resignation
(see page 49)

Acronym

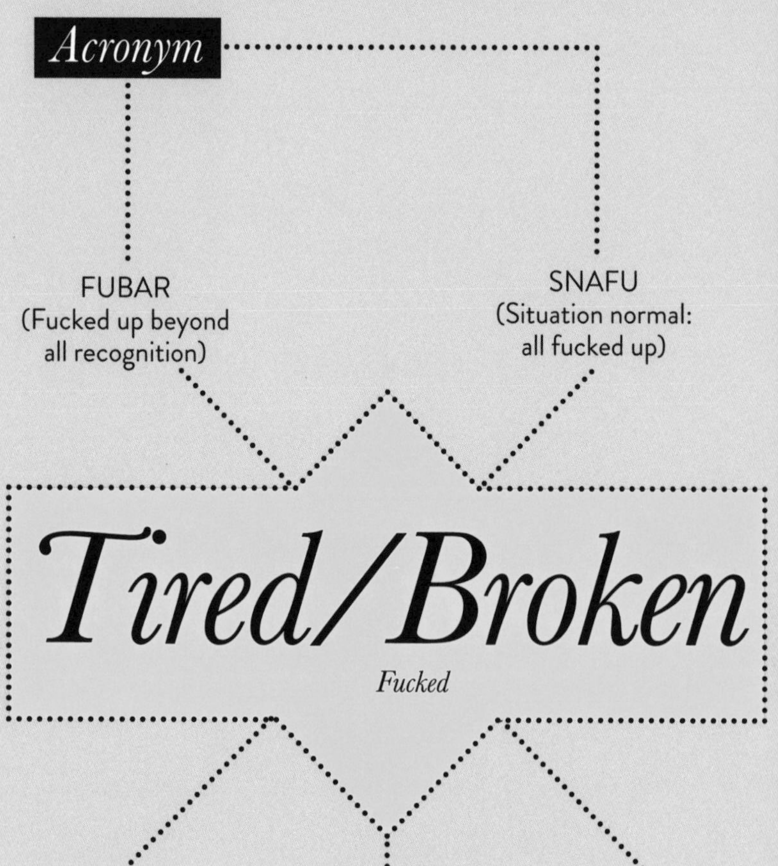
Acronym
FUBAR
(Fucked up beyond all recognition)
SNAFU
(Situation normal: all fucked up)
Tired/Broken
Fucked
It's fucked
Fucked up
I'm fucked

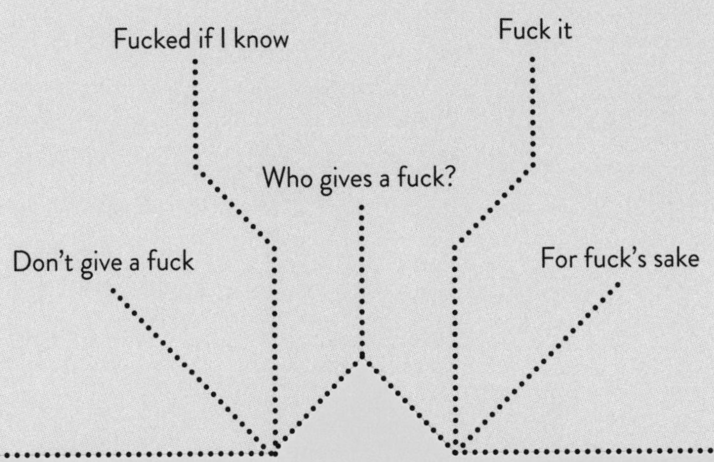

Resignation

Acceptance of something undesirable but inevitable

Fucking hell

Amazement

(see page 46)

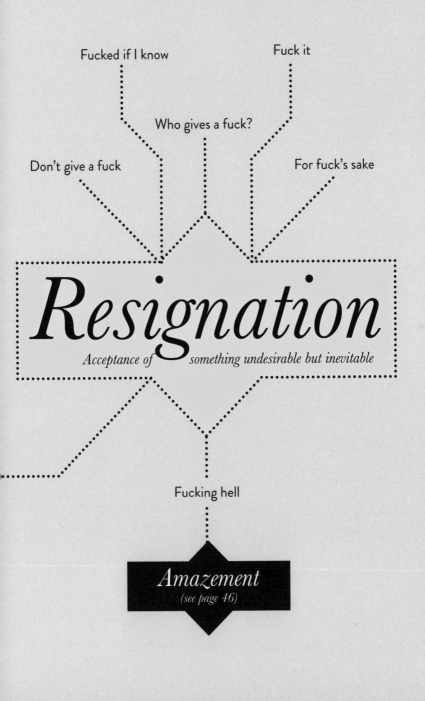

Chapter 2
{*Shit*}

Shit

Although as a noun, shit refers to fecal matter, it has many additional meanings; to defecate, something of little value, nonsense, or as an expression of surprise, or anger.

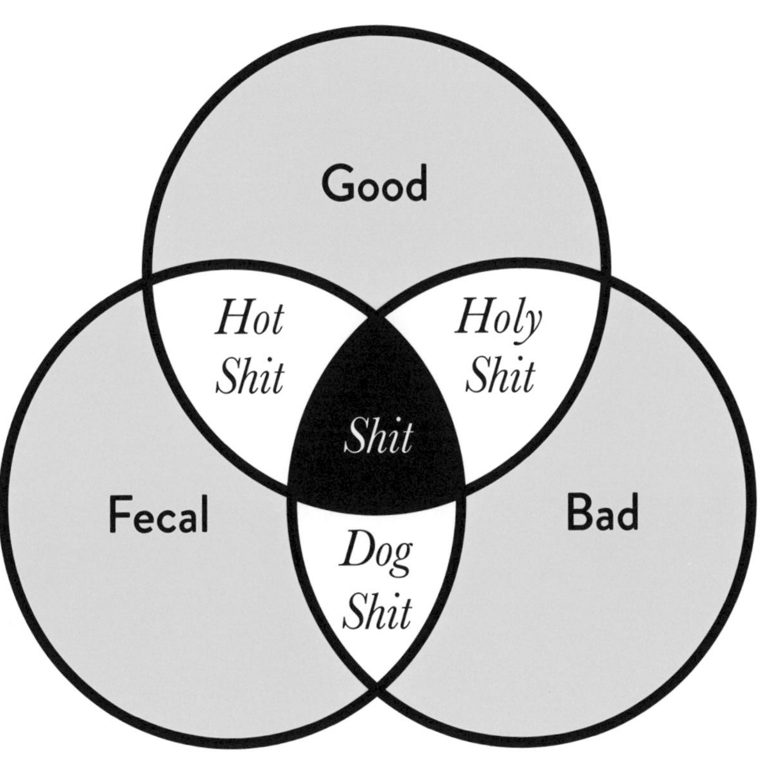
Good
Hot Shit
Holy Shit
Shit
Fecal
Bad
Dog Shit

Etymology

The origin of shit is shrouded in the steaming toilets of time, possibly derived from Old English, which had the nouns: **scite** (dung) and **scitte** (diarrhoea).

This eventually changed in Middle English to **schitte** (excrement), **schyt** (diarrhoea)

The word has several similars in modern Germanic languages:

German: **Scheiße**
Dutch: **schijt**
Swedish: **skit**
Icelandic: **skítur**

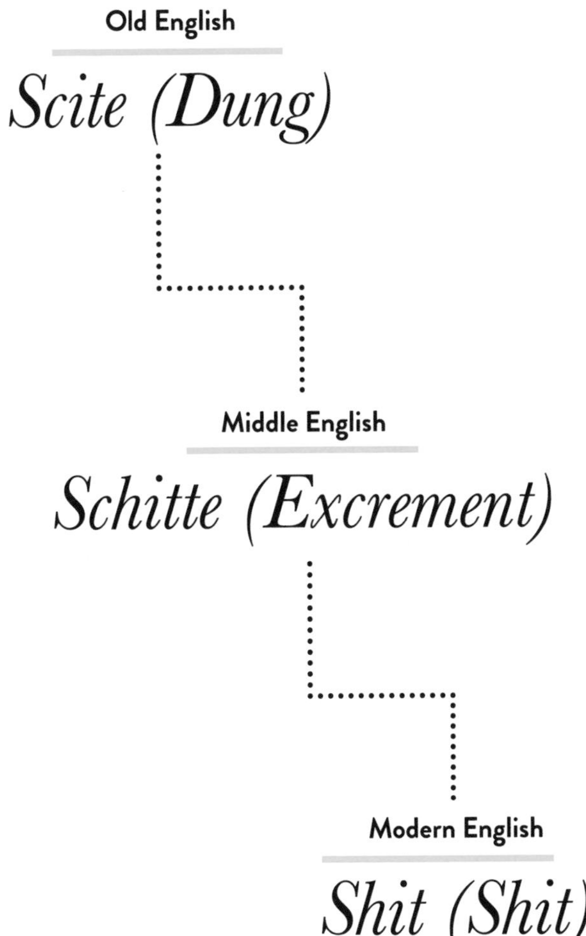
Old English
Scite (Dung)
Middle English
Schitte (Excrement)
Modern English
Shit (Shit)

Chapter 2

Punctuation

KNOW YOUR SHIT

OR KNOW YOU'RE SHIT

Shit as an adjective, verb and noun

Adjective

"The shitting shit...

Noun
(person)

Verb
(to defecate/faeces)

…shat on my shit"

Noun
(object)

Good shit

THIS IS GOOOOD SHIT

Bad shit

WE ARE IN SOME DEEP SHIT

Animal shit

Adding an animal before the word shit can vastly change its meaning.

Chicken shit = **Cowardice**
Dog shit = **Rubbish**
Apeshit = **Anger**

Bullshit = **Nonsense**
Horseshit = **Nonsense**
Batshit = **Crazy**

"Apeshit dog"

A mad dog

"Dogshit Ape"

A rubbish ape

Tenses

Tense	Meaning	Example
Simple past	She did it	She shat
Simple present	She usually does it	She shits
Past progressive	She was doing it at that time	She was shitting
Present progressive	She is doing it now	She is shitting
Past perfect	Before that time, she had already	She had shat
Present perfect	She has done it already	She has shitted
Future	She will do it	She will shit

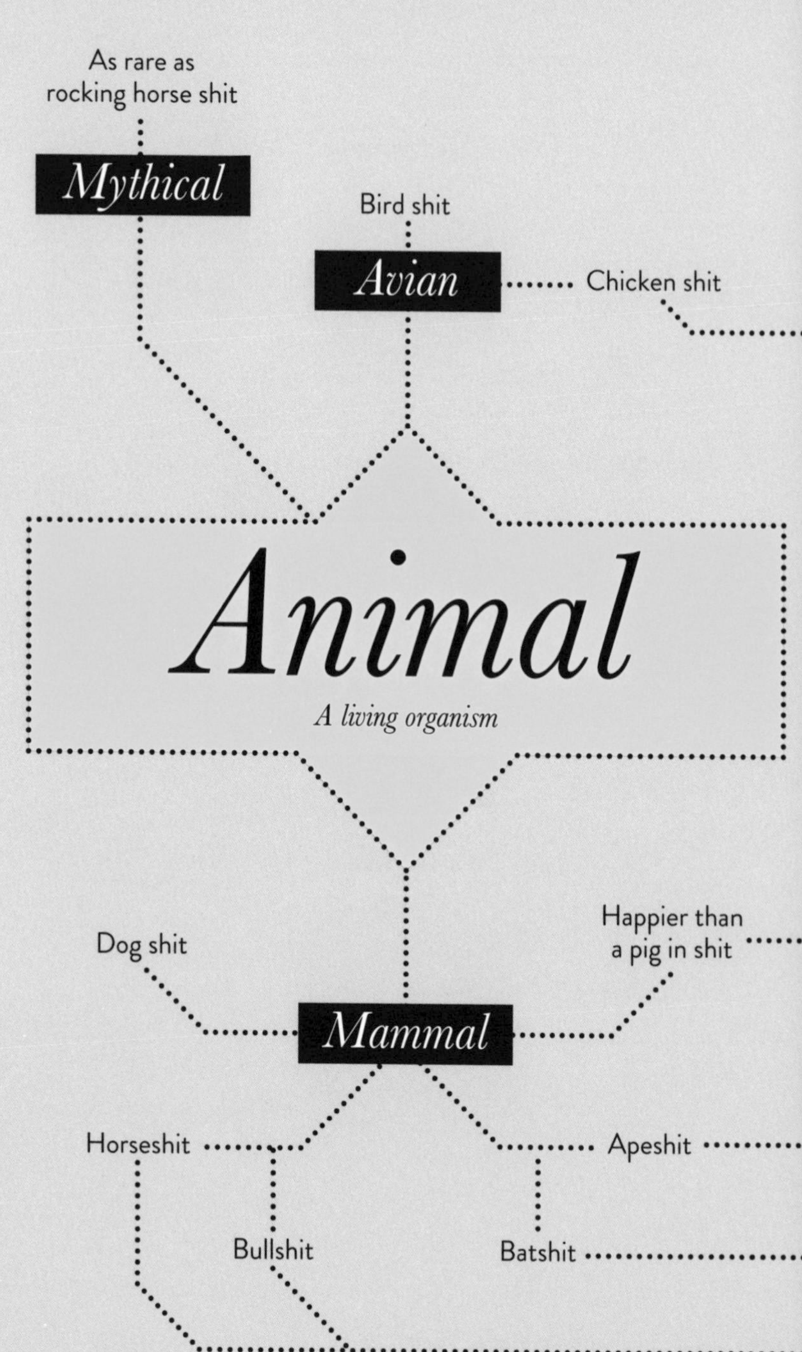
As rare as rocking horse shit
Mythical
Bird shit
Avian
Chicken shit
Animal
A living organism
Dog shit
Happier than a pig in shit
Mammal
Horseshit
Apeshit
Bullshit
Batshit

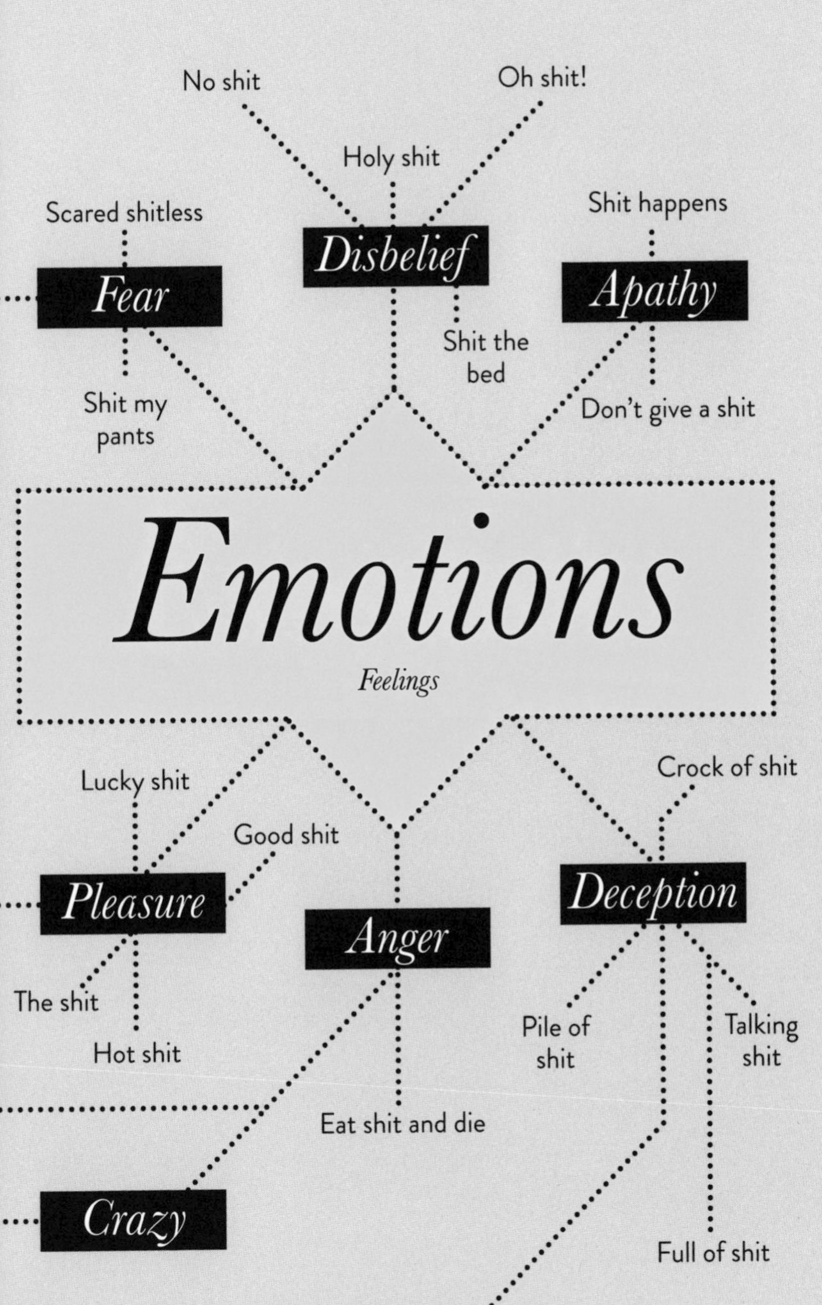
No shit
Oh shit!
Holy shit
Scared shitless
Disbelief
Shit happens
Fear
Apathy
Shit the bed
Shit my pants
Don't give a shit
Emotions
Feelings
Lucky shit
Crock of shit
Good shit
Pleasure
Deception
Anger
The shit
Pile of shit
Talking shit
Hot shit
Eat shit and die
Crazy
Full of shit

Shithead
Dumbshit
Shit for brains
Stupidity
A lack of good sense
No shit, Sherlock
Thick as shit
Dipshit

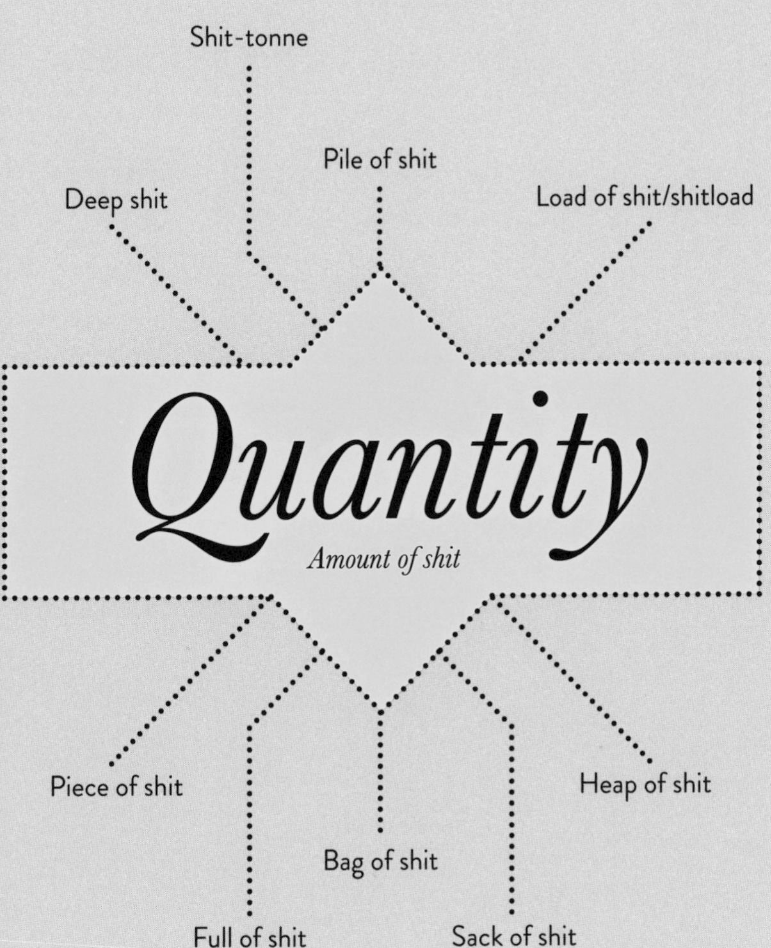
Shit-tonne
Pile of shit
Deep shit
Load of shit/shitload
Quantity
Amount of shit
Piece of shit
Heap of shit
Bag of shit
Full of shit
Sack of shit

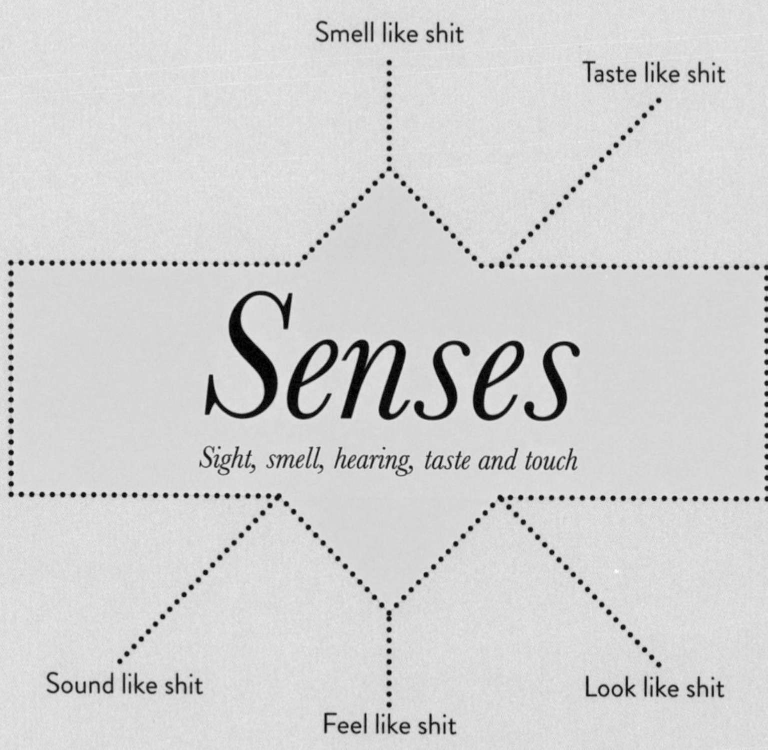
Smell like shit
Taste like shit
Senses
Sight, smell, hearing, taste and touch
Sound like shit
Feel like shit
Look like shit

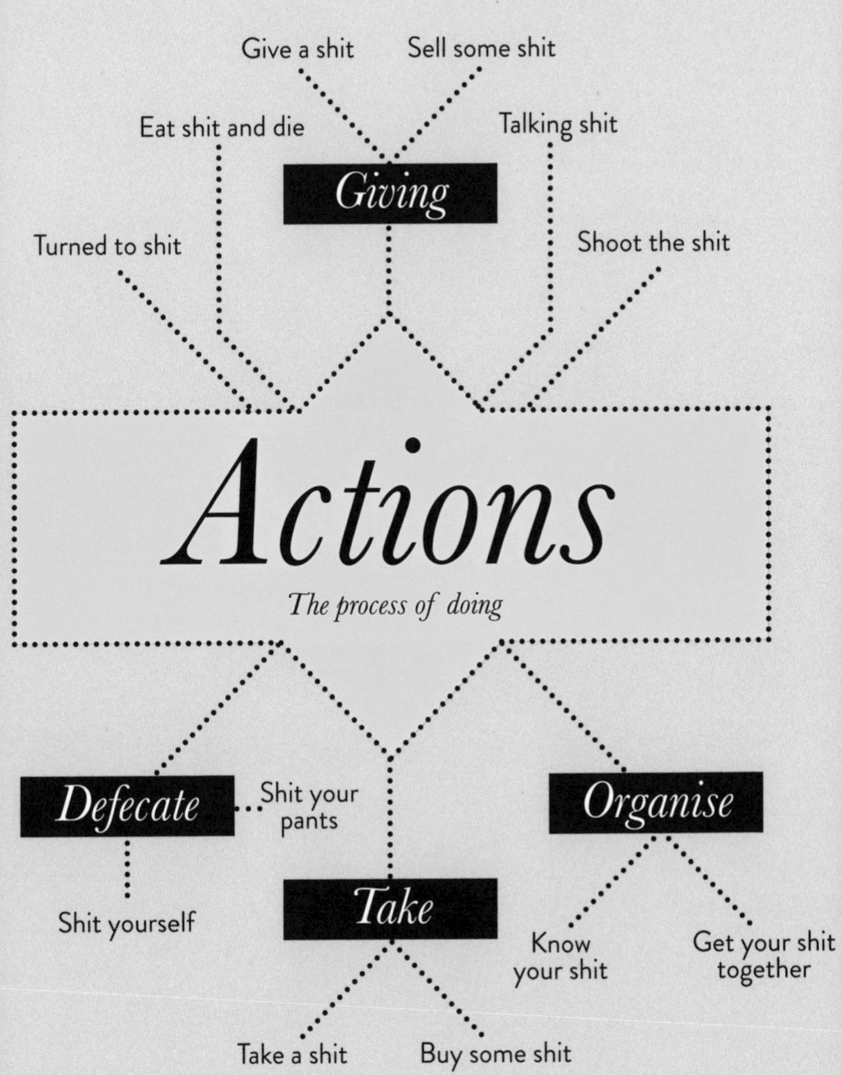
Give a shit
Sell some shit
Eat shit and die
Talking shit
Giving
Turned to shit
Shoot the shit
Actions
The process of doing
Defecate
Shit your pants
Organise
Shit yourself
Take
Know your shit
Get your shit together
Take a shit
Buy some shit

Shit creek
without a paddle
Shit out of luck
Deep shit
Bad News
An unwelcome development
Shitstorm
Oh shit
Turned to shit

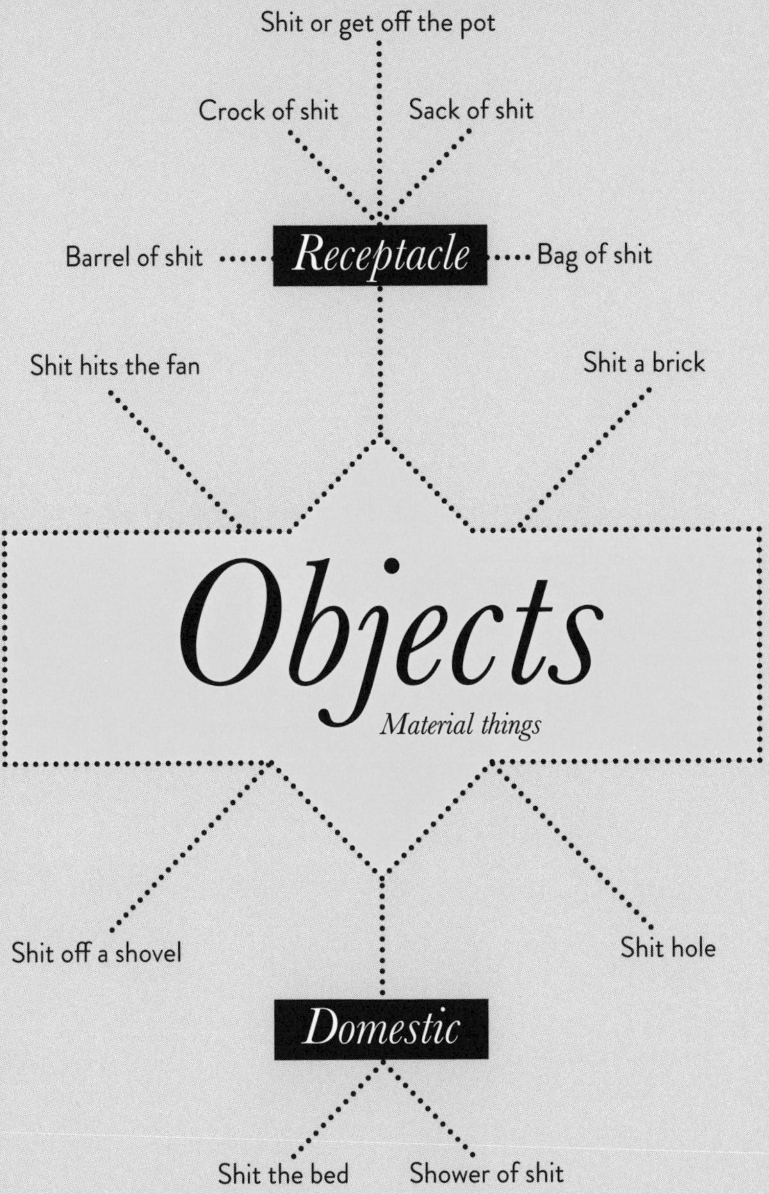

Shit or get off the pot

Crock of shit

Sack of shit

Barrel of shit

Receptacle

Bag of shit

Shit hits the fan

Shit a brick

Objects

Material things

Shit off a shovel

Shit hole

Domestic

Shit the bed

Shower of shit

Chapter 3
{Piss}

Piss

A slang term for urine (a sterile liquid produced by the kidneys of many animals).

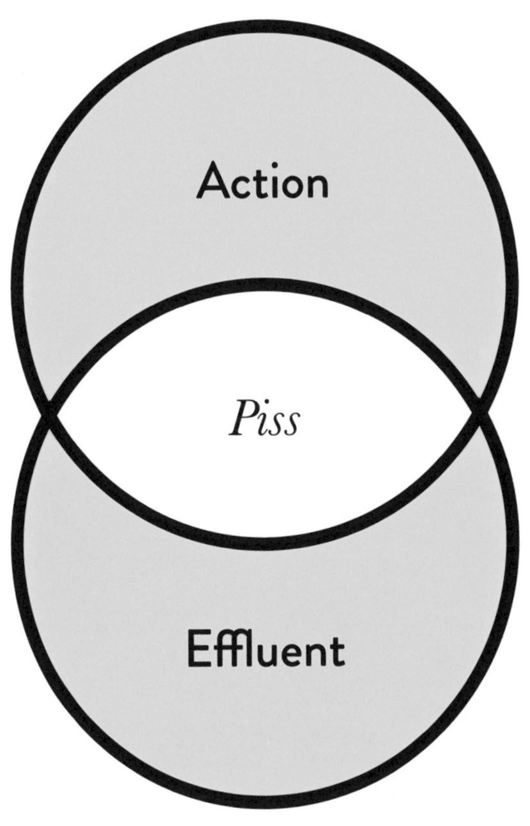
Action
Piss
Effluent

Etymology

Piss comes from the Old French word **pisser**. Both words are onomatopoeic for the sound of urination. Mostly used before the fourteenth century, before being replaced with the more clinical term, **urinate**. Piss is now considered a vulgar term.

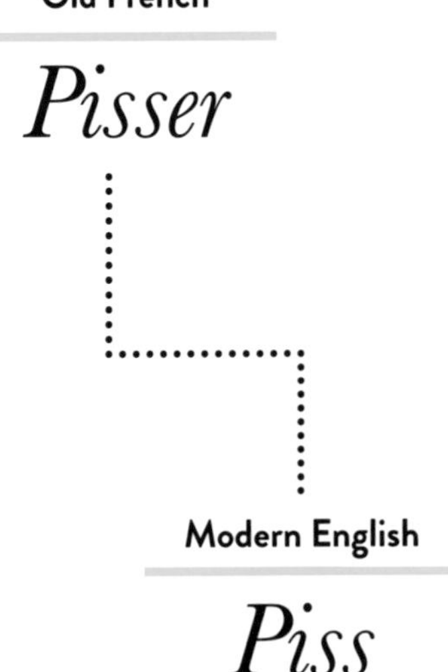
Old French
Pisser
Modern English
Piss

Piss as an adjective, verb and noun

Verb

"I'm pissed off - it's...

Verb
Noun
...pissing down with pissy piss"
Adjective

Context

As with many vulgar words context is everything. If we take a phrase like **pissed all over it**, it could mean that you literally urinated over an item, or figuratively that an activity was very easy or you have a superior skill or talent.

This tea tastes like piss!

Literal Sense	**Figurative Sense**
Urinating over an object	The activity was easy
"Pissed all over it"	*"Pissed all over it"*
Urinating in your clothes	Laughing
"Pissed myself"	*"Pissed myself"*

Tenses

The grammar around piss and its tenses is more complicated because of the three central meanings of piss (being drunk, being angry and urinating).

	Past	Present
Verb	Pissed	Pisses
Participle	Pissed	Pissing

	Tense	Meaning
I was pissed	Past	Intoxication
I was pissed	Past	Anger
I was pissing	Past	Urination
I am pissed	Present	Intoxication
I am pissed	Present	Anger
I am pissing	Present	Urination
I will be pissed	Future	Intoxication
I will be pissed	Future	Anger
I will be pissing	Present	Urination

Easy

PIECE OF PISS

Hard

PISSING IN THE WIND

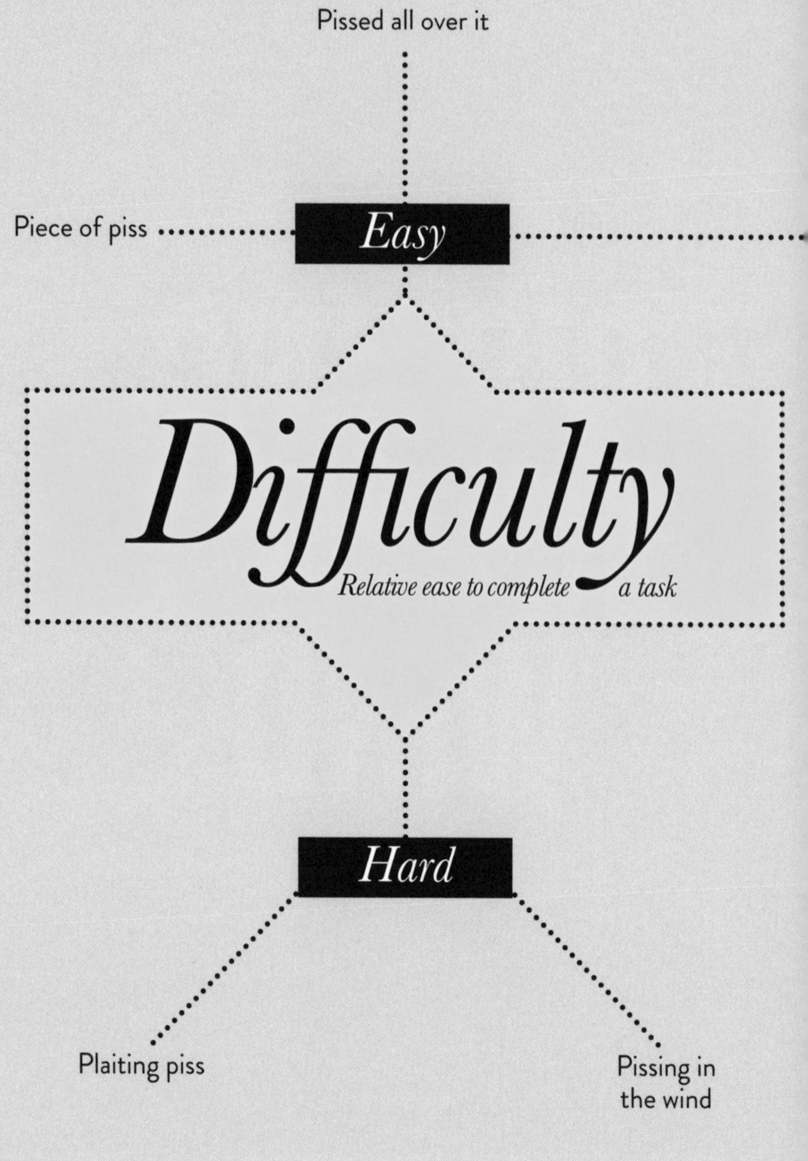

Pissed all over it

Piece of piss

Easy

Difficulty

Relative ease to complete a task

Hard

Plaiting piss

Pissing in the wind

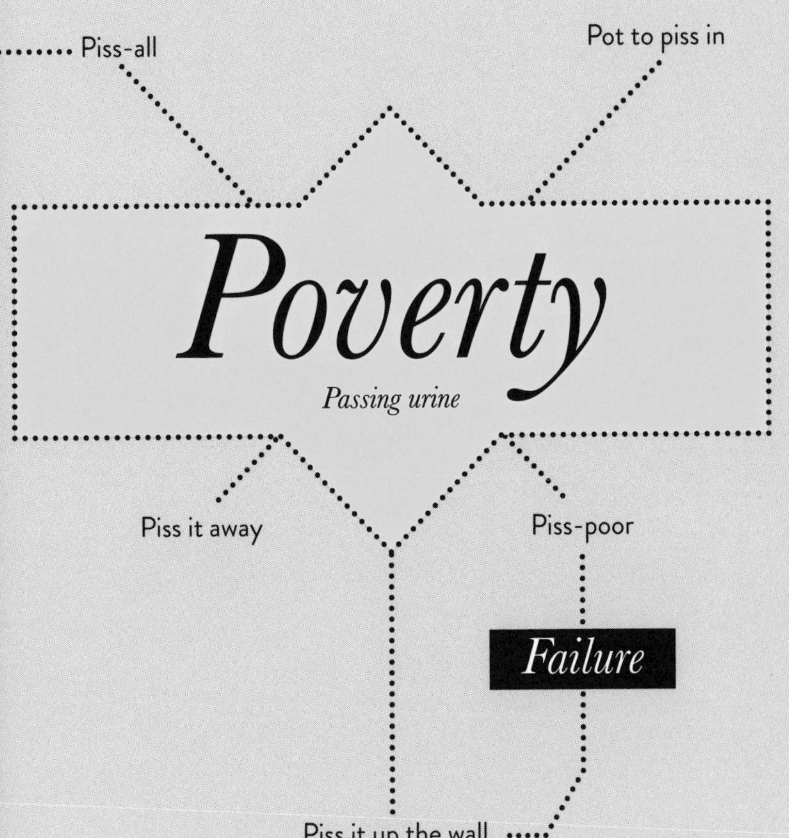
Piss-all
Pot to piss in
Poverty
Passing urine
Piss it away
Piss-poor
Failure
Piss it up the wall

Pissed as a fart

Pissed as a newt

Pissed off

Drunk

Being pissed

On the piss

All pissed up

Piss up

Pisshead

Piss artist

Insults

(see page 90)

Cat's piss

Animals

Rat's piss

Beer

Alcoholic beverage

Tramp's piss

Warm piss

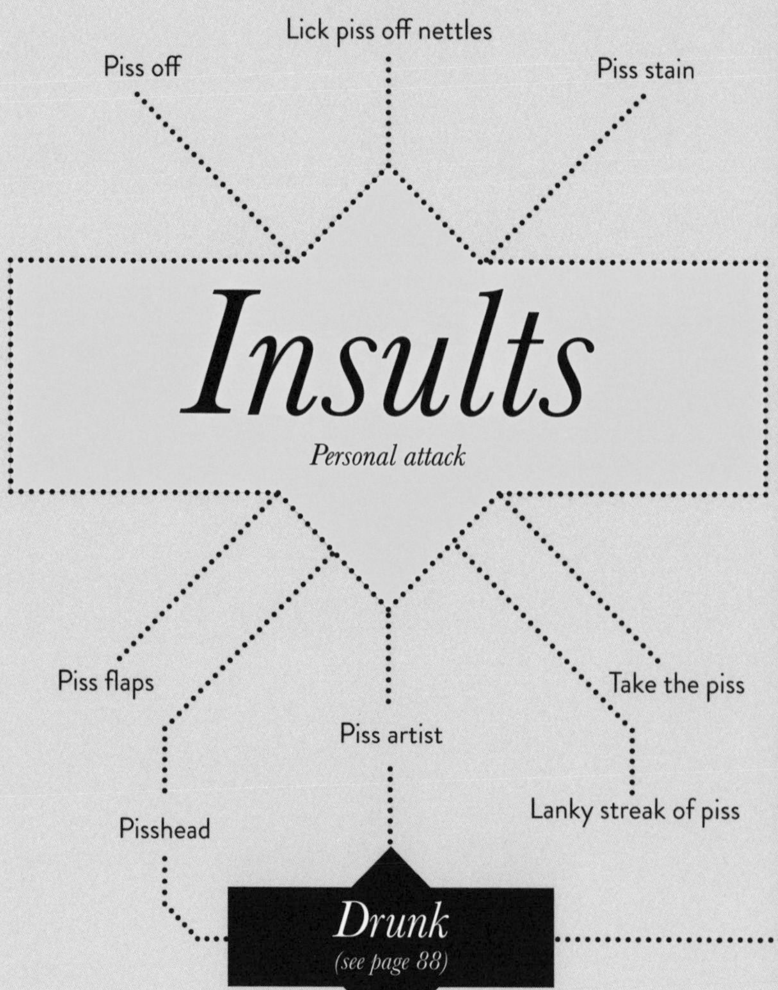
Lick piss off nettles
Piss off
Piss stain
Insults
Personal attack
Piss flaps
Take the piss
Piss artist
Lanky streak of piss
Pisshead
Drunk
(see page 88)

Pissing it down

The pissing rain

Precipitation

Rain

Being pissed on

Pissed off

Anger

Strong annoyance or hostility

Pissed

Pissy

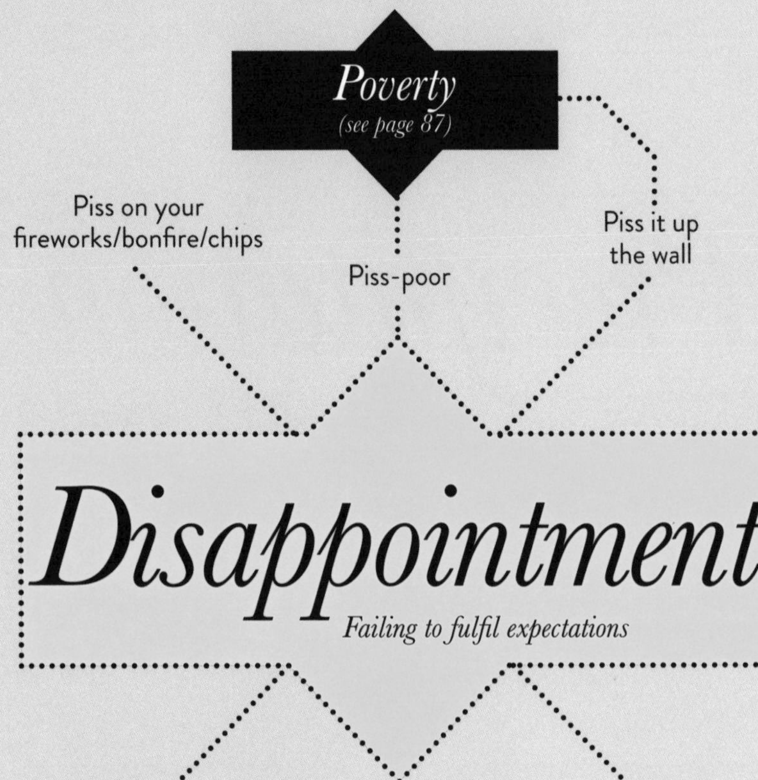
Poverty
(see page 87)
Piss on your fireworks/bonfire/chips
Piss-poor
Piss it up the wall
Disappointment
Failing to fulfil expectations
Piss-take
Pisser

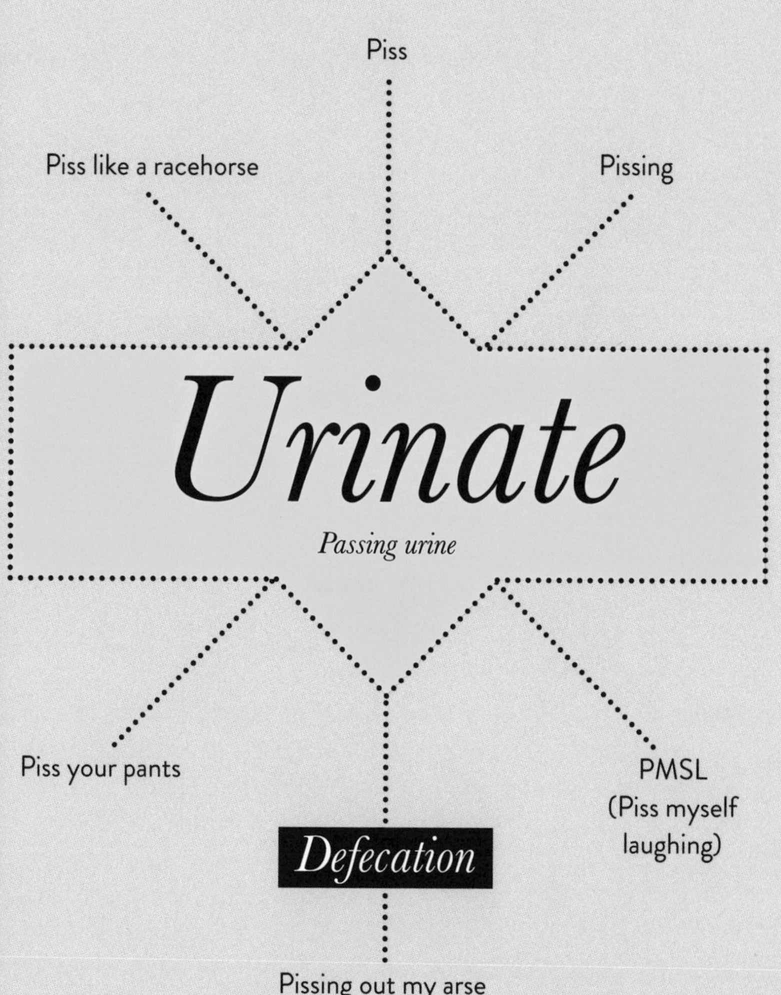

Pissing out my arse

Chapter 4

{*Bollocks*}

Bollocks

A useful word to express something of poor quality, nonsense or the male gonads. A word slightly less offensive than bullshit to use when someone is talking bollocks.

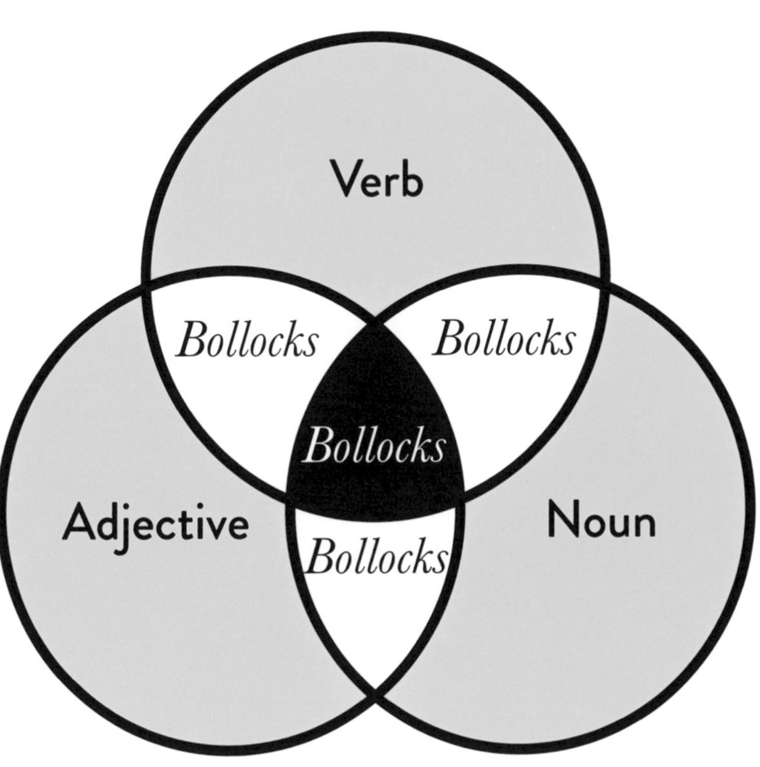

N.B. It's all bollocks.

Etymology

Bollocks derives from the Old English word for testicles, **ballokes**. The term was used in everyday language as the word for testicles and only became offensive in the mid-seventeenth century.

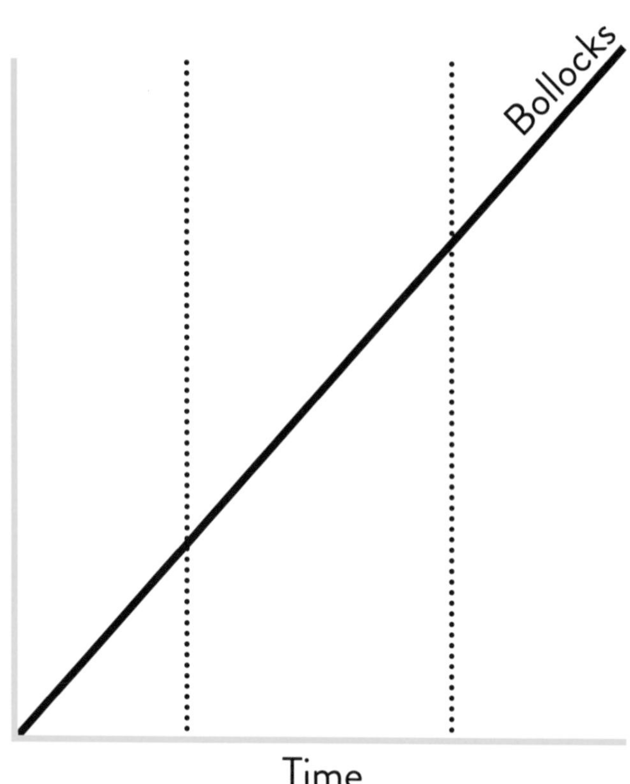

Old English

Ballokes

Middle English

Ballocks

Modern English

Bollocks

Bollocks as an interjection, verb and noun

Interjection

"Oh bollocks, I bollocked...

Verb

Noun

…him for talking bollocks, out of his bollocks"

Noun

Good DOG'S BOLLOCKS

Bad

COMPLETE BOLLOCKS

NEVER MIND THE BOLLOCKS

HERE'S THE SEX PISTOLS

Never Mind the Bollocks is the title of the only studio album released by the Sex Pistols, on 28 October 1977.

The band had appeared on live TV and famously swore at host Bill Grundy, calling him:

"You dirty sod...
You dirty old man...
You dirty bastard...
You dirty fucker...
What a fucking rotter"

Because the album's title contained the word **bollocks** it was deemed offensive. Some record charts refused to list the album. In its place was just a blank space, or in other words, bollocks all.

Breasticles and Testicles

Breasts and testes share many euphemistic roots.

Food		’ers	
Testicles	Breasts	Testicles	Breasts
Acorns	Apples	Conkers	Bangers
Grapes	Baps	Danglers	Boulders
Jaffas	Chest potatoes	Knackers	Hooters
Kiwis	Coconuts	Slappers	Knockers
Meatballs	Fried eggs		
Nuts	Melons		
Plums	Spuds		
Prunes			
Spuds			
Tater tots			
Two veg			
Walnuts			

Spheres

Testicles	Breasts
Balls	Love orbs
Marbles	Mounds
Rocks	
Stones	

Receptacles

Testicles	Breasts
Ballbag	Fun bags
Ballsack	Jugs
Chickenskin handbag	Cans
Coin purse	
Hairy beanbag	

Nonsense

Testicles	Breasts
Goolies	Gazongas
	Yaboos
	Wabs
	Ta-Tas

Polite/medical

Testicles	Breasts
Family jewels	Breasts
Privates	Mammaries
Testes	Bust
Scrotum	Bosoms
Gonads	Chest
Nads	

Bullshit or Bollocks?

At first glance, bullshit and bollocks seem to have a similar meaning, but there is a crucial difference.

When someone is talking bollocks they are not aware that they are using untruths. Whereas when talking bullshit, the bullshitter is well aware that they are in fact talking bullshit.

You're talking bollocks
Bullshit!

Bullshit

"I climbed Mount Everest"

Bollocks

"Mount Everest is in Peru"

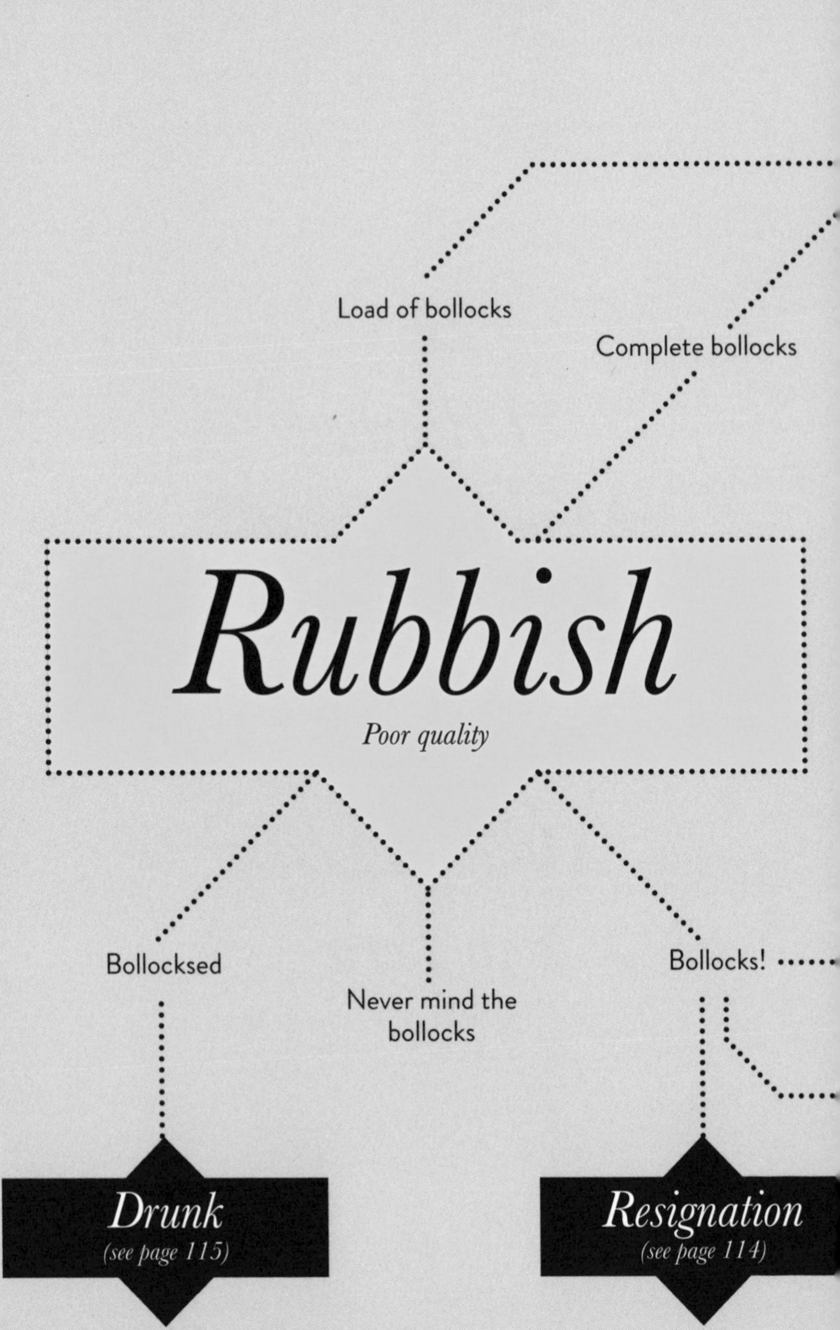

Load of bollocks

Complete bollocks

Rubbish

Poor quality

Bollocksed

Never mind the bollocks

Bollocks!

Drunk
(see page 115)

Resignation
(see page 114)

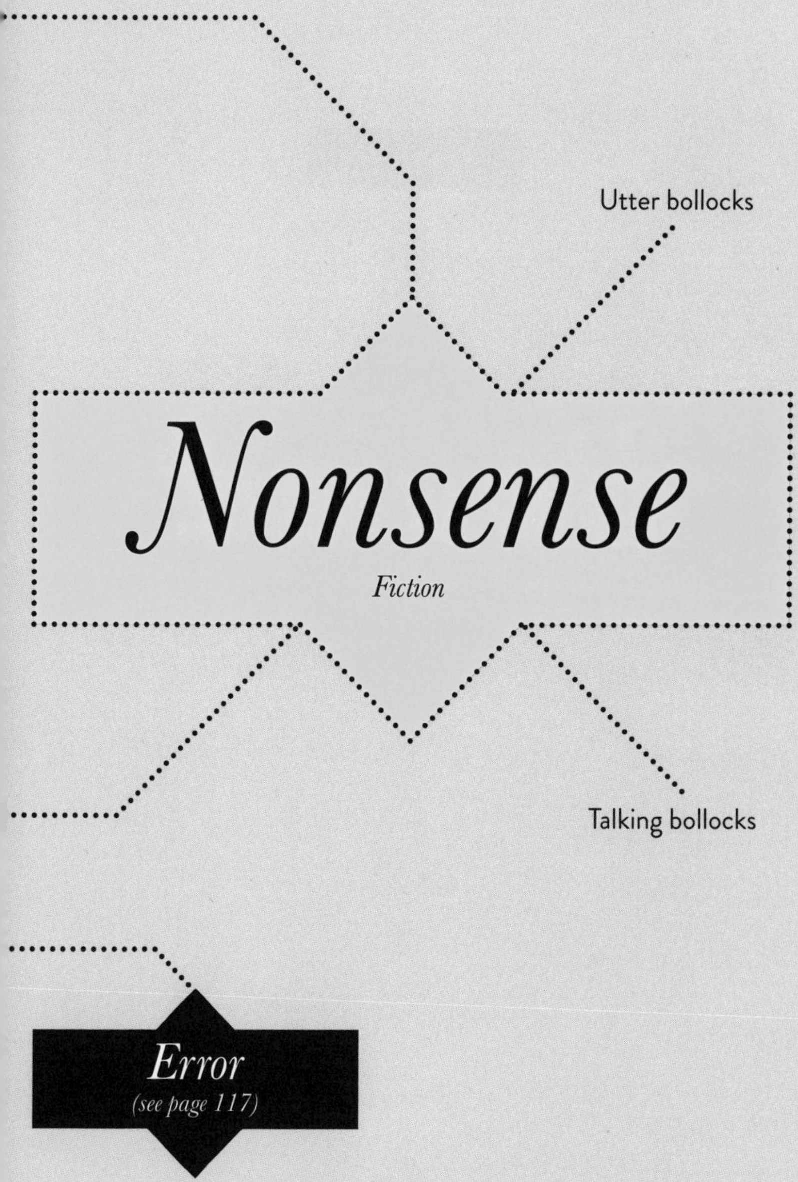

Utter bollocks

Nonsense

Fiction

Talking bollocks

Error
(see page 117)

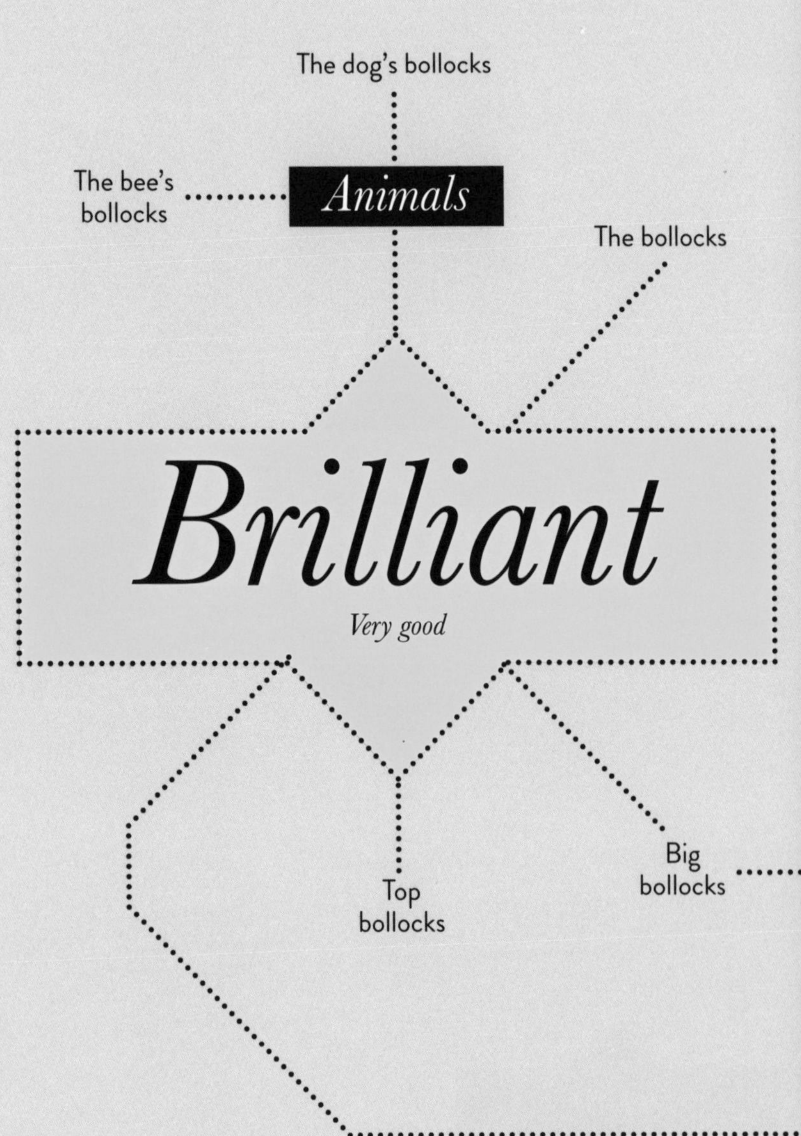
The dog's bollocks
The bee's bollocks
Animals
The bollocks
Brilliant
Very good
Top bollocks
Big bollocks

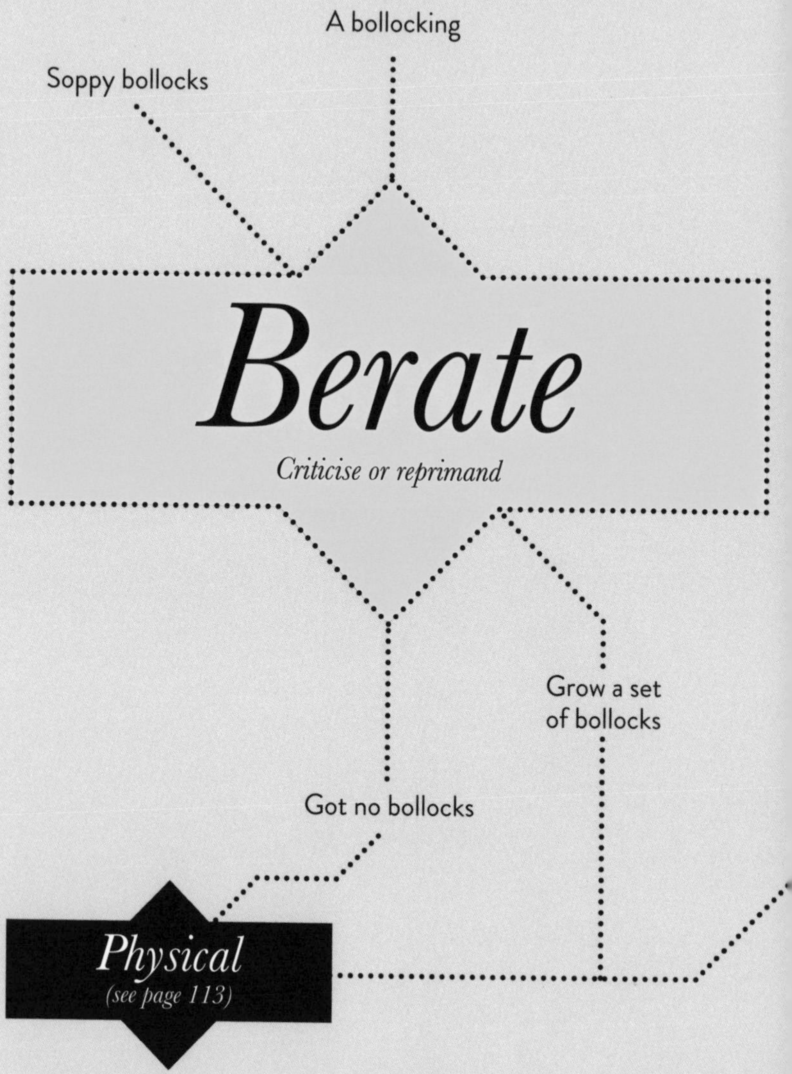

A bollocking

Soppy bollocks

Berate

Criticise or reprimand

Grow a set of bollocks

Got no bollocks

Physical

(see page 113)

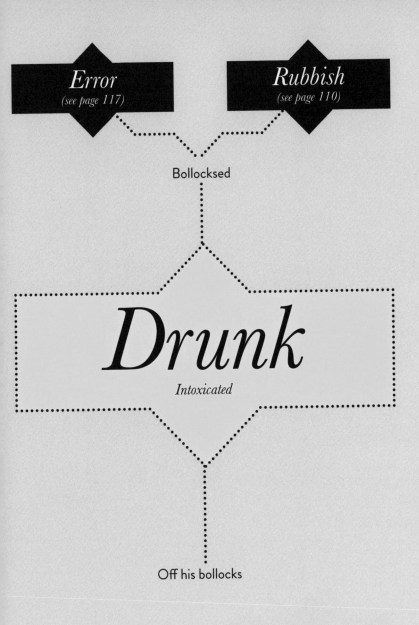

Error
(see page 117)

Rubbish
(see page 110)

Bollocksed

Drunk

Intoxicated

Off his bollocks

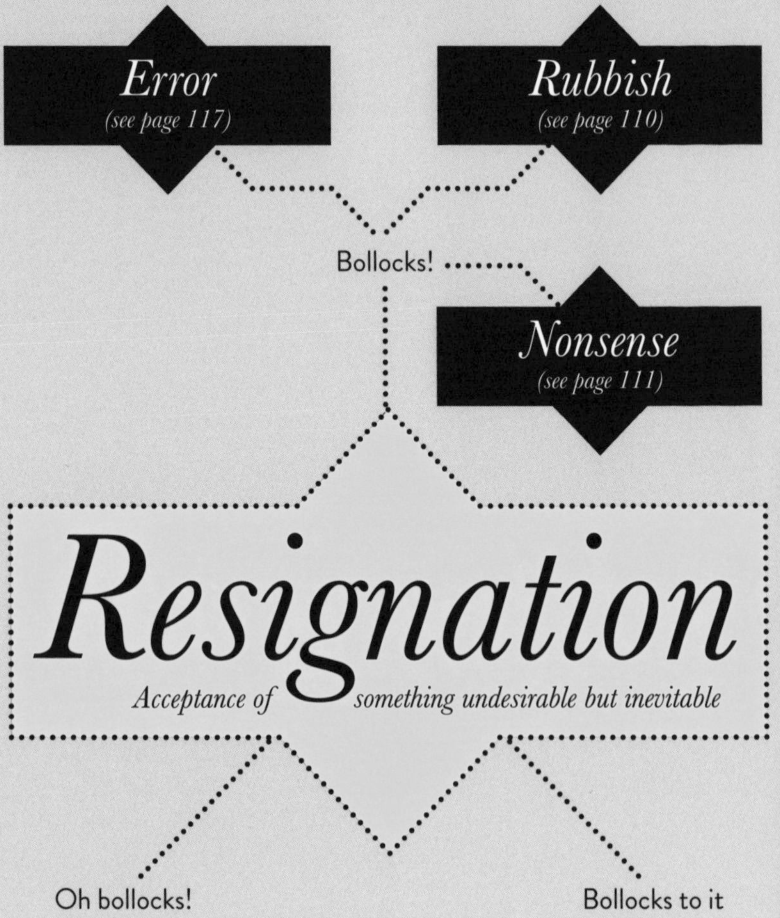

Error
(see page 117)

Rubbish
(see page 110)

Bollocks!

Nonsense
(see page 111)

Resignation

Acceptance of something undesirable but inevitable

Oh bollocks!

Bollocks to it

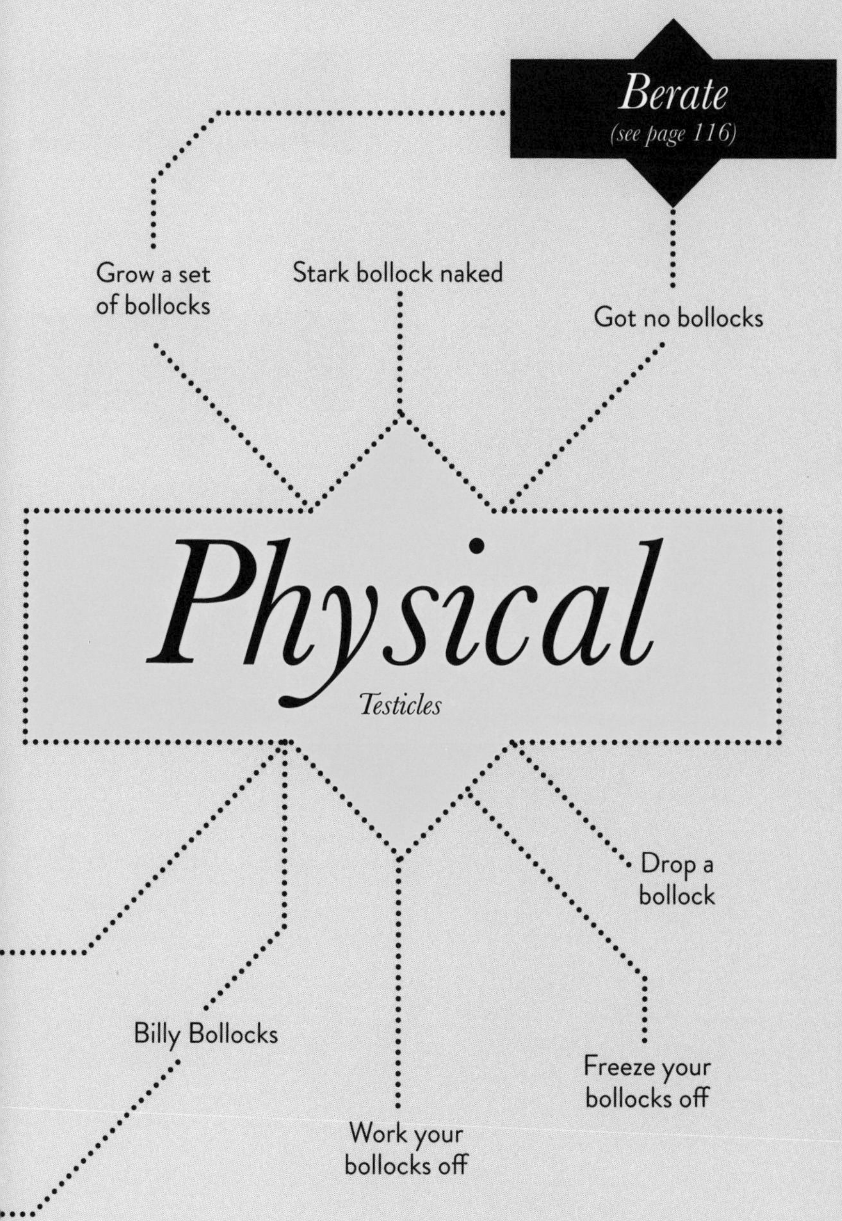

Berate
(see page 116)

Grow a set of bollocks

Stark bollock naked

Got no bollocks

Physical

Testicles

Drop a bollock

Billy Bollocks

Freeze your bollocks off

Work your bollocks off

Error

A mistake

Bollocksed

Drop a bollock

Bollocks up

Bollocks!

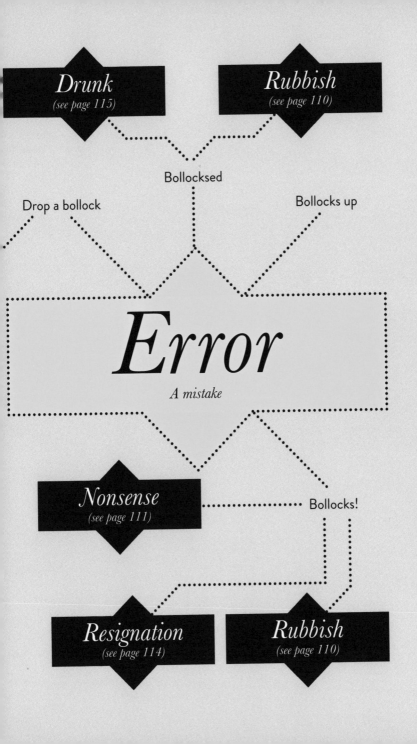

Drunk
(see page 115)

Rubbish
(see page 110)

Nonsense
(see page 111)

Resignation
(see page 114)

Rubbish
(see page 110)

Chapter 5
{*Arse*}

Arse

A person's buttocks or anus. Can also refer to someone behaving in a silly manner.

In the US, **ass** is used to describe the above definition as well as a donkey and it can be interchangeable (eg. 'you're an ass'). But in the UK, **ass** is mainly used to refer to donkeys.

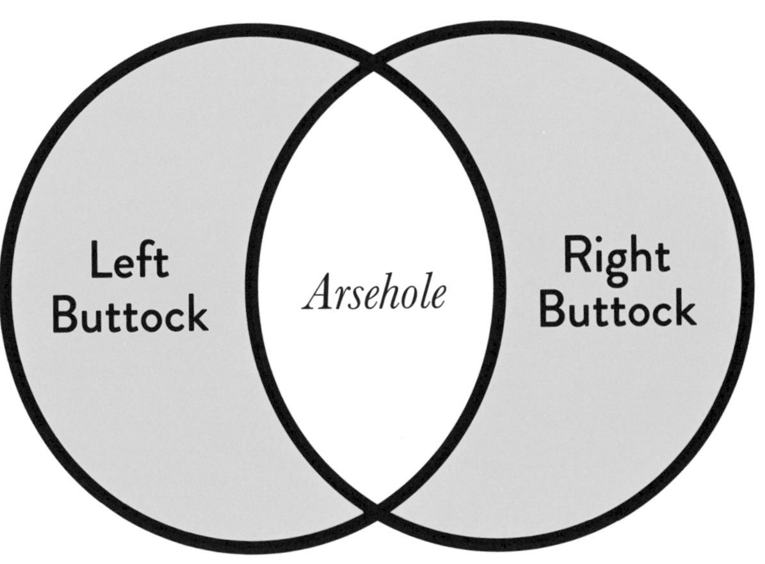
Left Buttock
Arsehole
Right Buttock

Etymology

Arse has Germanic roots and is related closely to the modern Dutch and German words for arse.

Lick me in the arse

Mozart, 1782

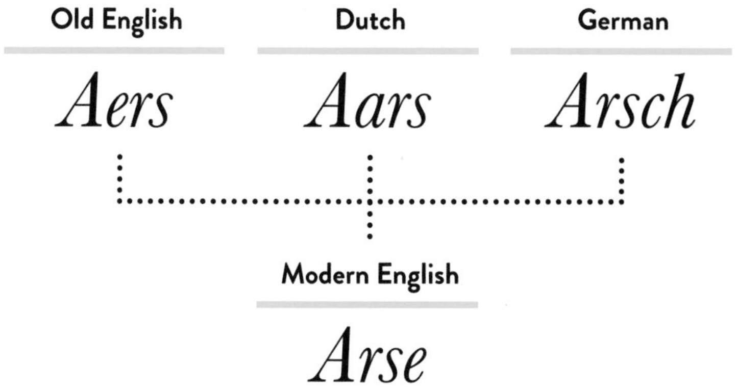

Old English	Dutch	German
Aers	*Aars*	*Arsch*

Modern English

Arse

Arse as an adjective, verb and noun

Adjective

"What an arsey arse - he couldn't...

Noun

Verb

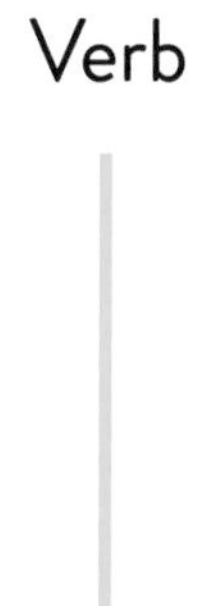

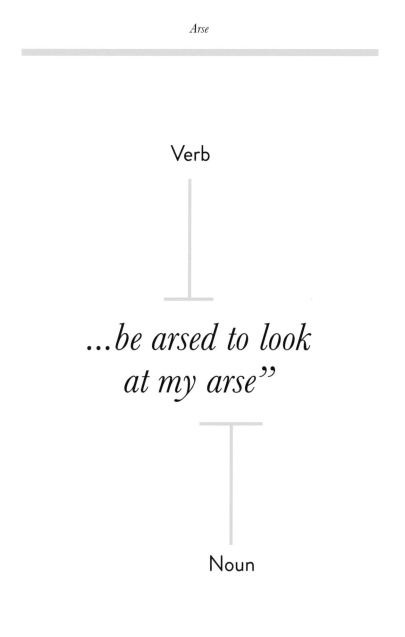

…be arsed to look at my arse"

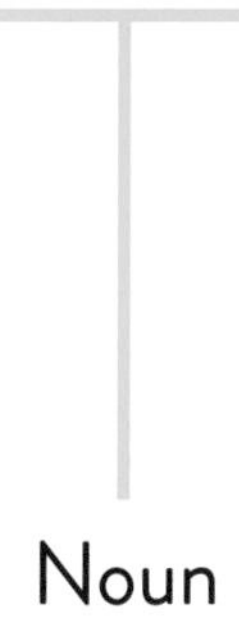

Noun

Smart-arse
Nice arse
Great arse
Good
Not bad
Kickass
Arse-kisser/licker
Piece of arse

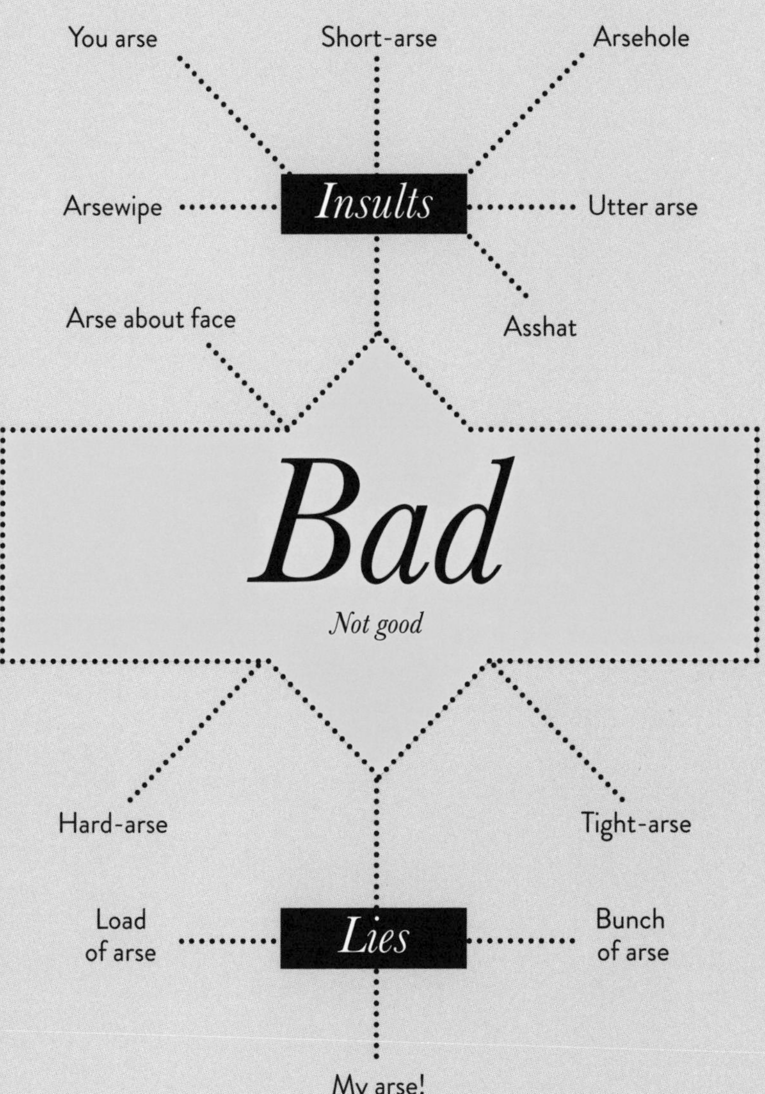
You arse
Short-arse
Arsehole
Arsewipe
Insults
Utter arse
Arse about face
Asshat
Bad
Not good
Hard-arse
Tight-arse
Load of arse
Lies
Bunch of arse
My arse!

Rat arsed

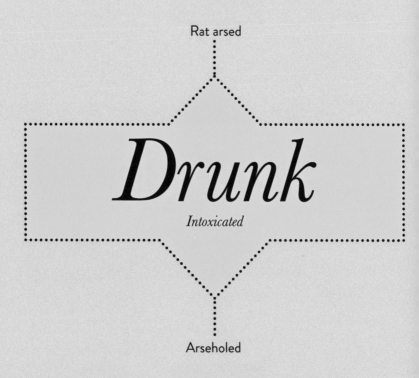

Drunk

Intoxicated

Arseholed

Arse over tit
Knowing your arse from your elbow
Dumb-arse
Idiocy
Not smart
Can't find arse with both hands
Arse about face
Jackass
Silly-arse

Running around like
a blue-arsed fly
Move your arse
Kick up the arse
Activity
Doing things
Arse about
Arse around
Can't be arsed
Half-arsed
Lazy-arse
Sit on your arse

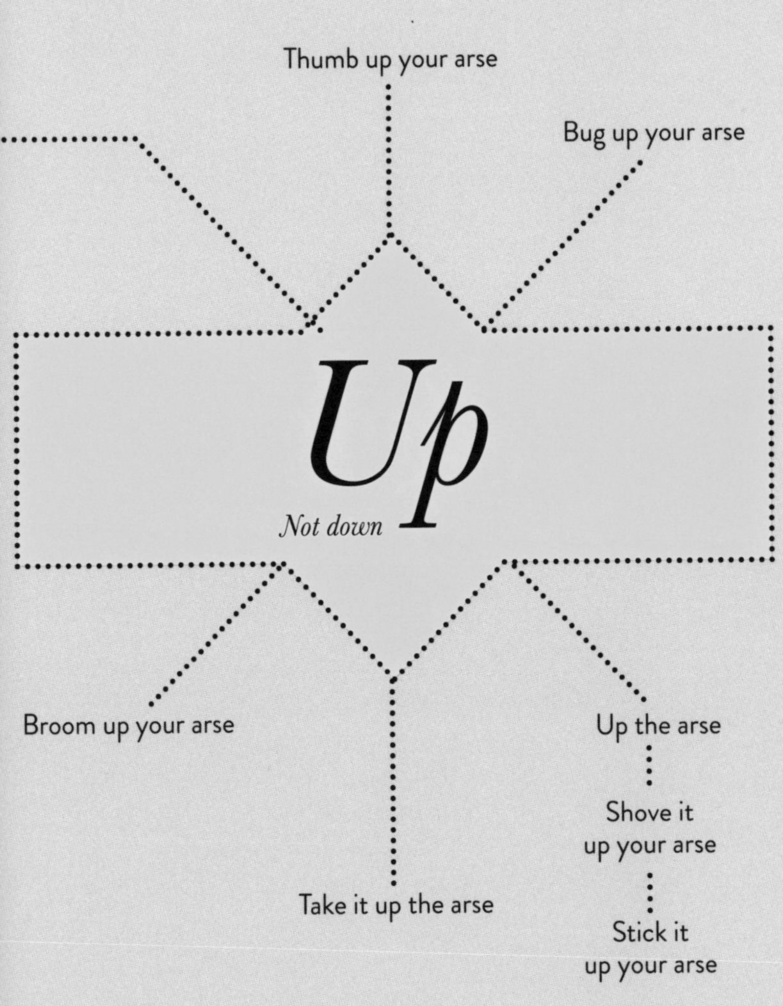
Thumb up your arse
Bug up your arse
Up
Not down
Broom up your arse
Up the arse
Shove it up your arse
Take it up the arse
Stick it up your arse

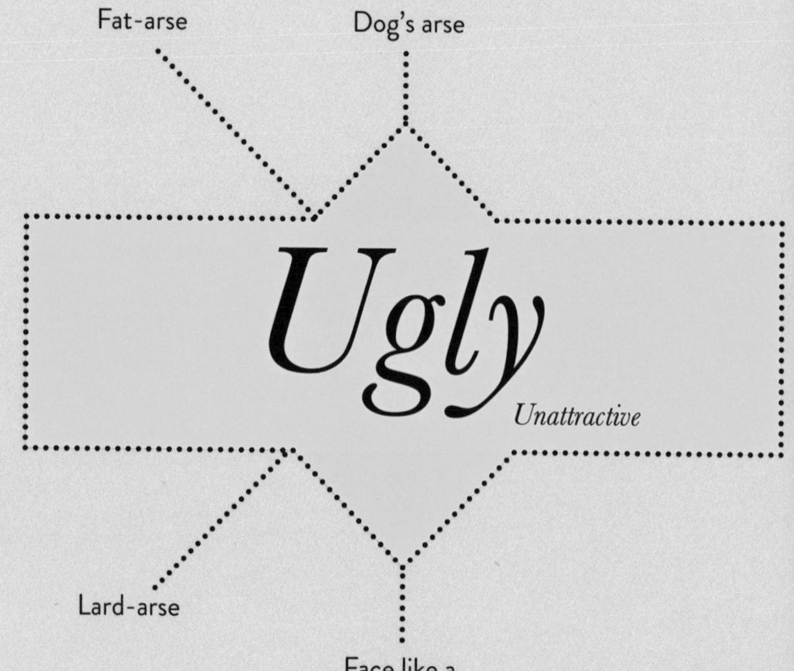
Fat-arse
Dog's arse
Ugly
Unattractive
Lard-arse
Face like a smacked arse

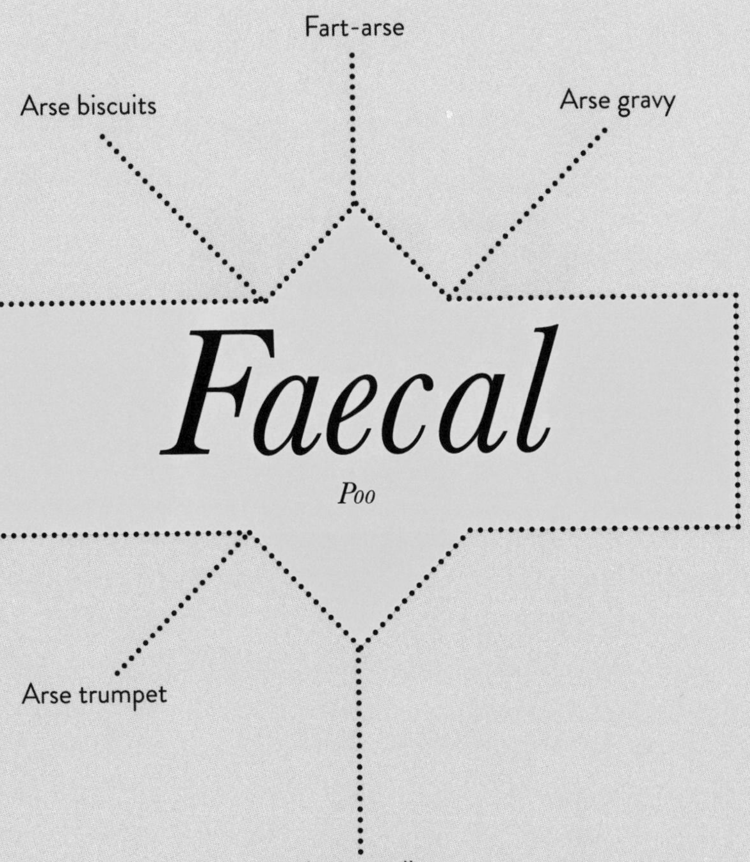
Fart-arse
Arse biscuits
Arse gravy
Faecal
Poo
Arse trumpet
Arse candle

JESUS LOVES YOU

BUT I THINK YOU'RE AN ARSEHOLE

Chapter 6

{*Dick*}

Dick

Dick is fairly limited in that it can refer directly to the penis, or to someone being foolish or idiotic.

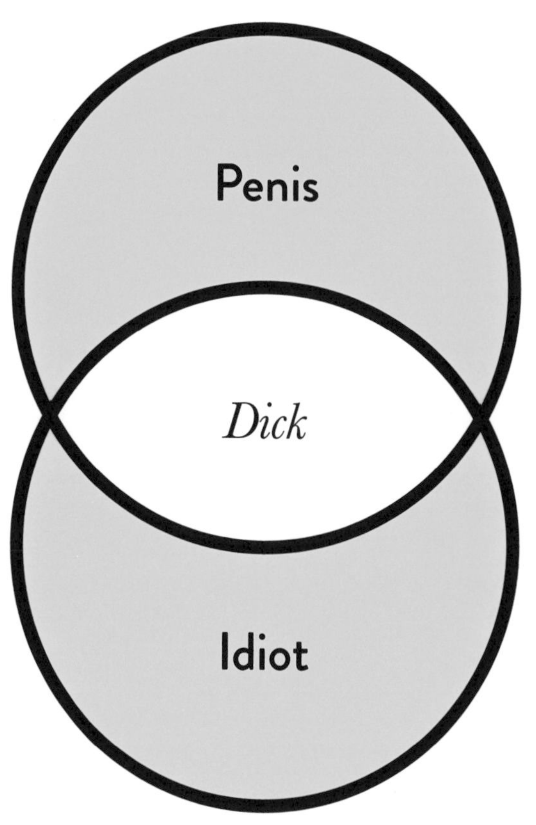
Penis
Dick
Idiot

Dick as a verb and noun

"He is such a dickhead...

...dicking around with his dick out"

Etymology

Dick is derived from the name Richard. Shortened to Rick, which then became Dick. It was used to refer to an everyman, and eventually to refer to an unsavoury character. It was only in the 1880s that military slang began using dick to refer to the penis.

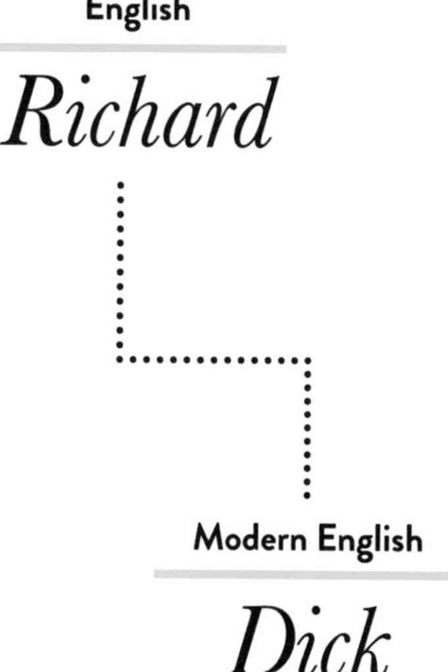
English
Richard
Modern English
Dick

Detective

Dick

Penis

Cock

Dickhead

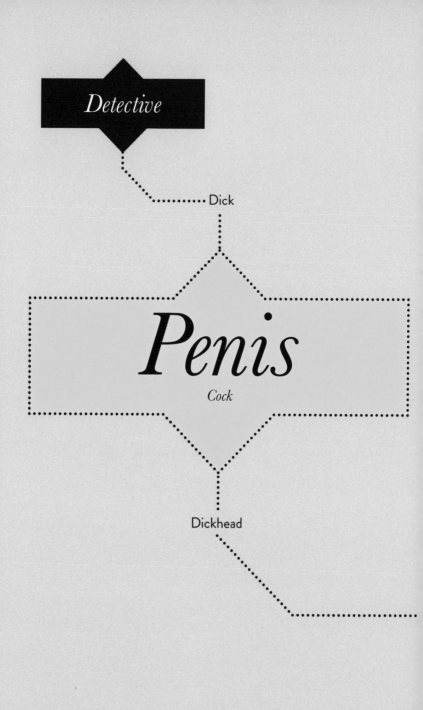

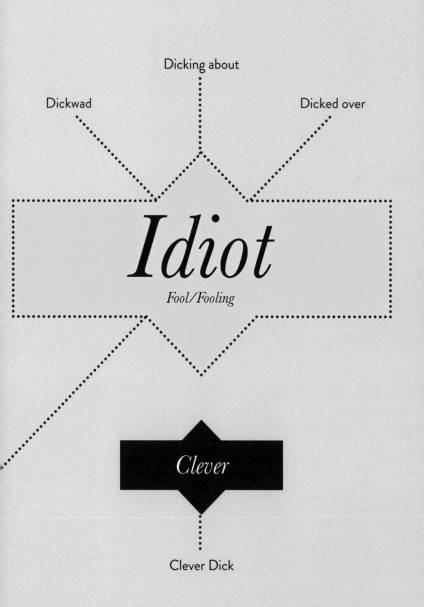

Dicking about

Dickwad

Dicked over

Idiot

Fool/Fooling

Clever Dick

Chapter 7

{*Cunt*}

Cunt

Cunt is a vulgar word for female genitalia, also used to mean an unpleasant or stupid person. Cunt is currently the most offensive word in the English language and one of the last words that still has the power to shock.

London and Oxford both have a Gropecunte Lane, a former red light district. It became taboo towards the end of the eighteenth century, and unprintable until the late twentieth century.

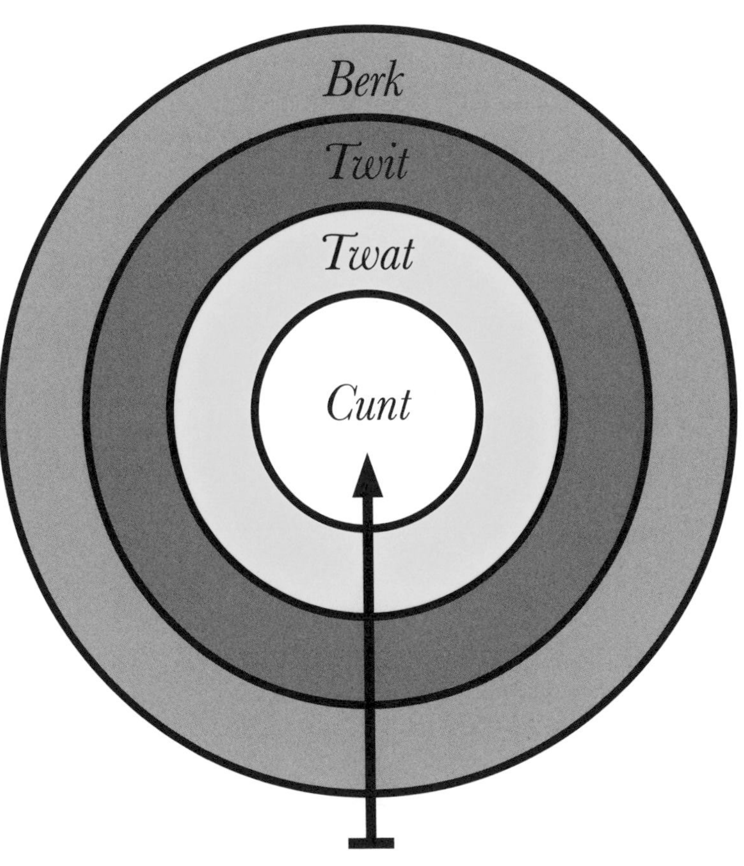
Berk
Twit
Twat
Cunt
Level of Offensiveness

Cunt as an adjective, verb and noun

Adjective

"He's being a cunting cunt...

Noun

...because I got cunted"

Etymology

Cunt is related to **Kunta** in Norwegian and Swedish dialects and **Kunte** in German, Middle Dutch and Danish dialects.

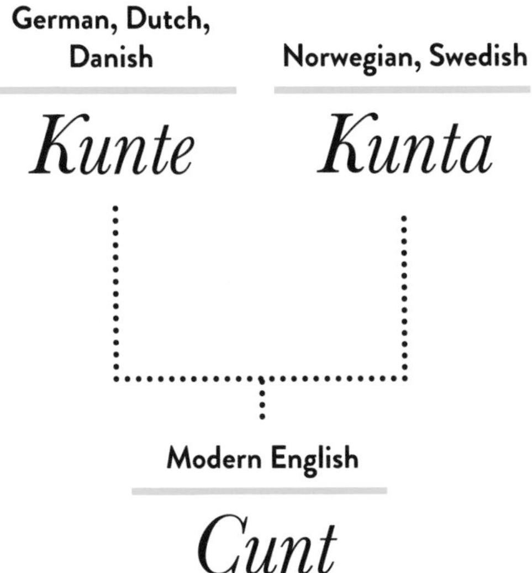
German, Dutch, Danish
Kunte
Norwegian, Swedish
Kunta
Modern English
Cunt

Genitals in the strongest terms

In 2016, Ofcom compiled a list of the most offensive words in the English language. Synonyms for genitalia make up most of the "strong" sections, with female genitalia dominating.

Mild

Arse
Bloody
Bugger
Cow
Crap
Damn
Ginger
Git
God
Goddam
Jesus Christ
Minger
Sod off

Medium

Arsehole
Balls
Bint
Bitch
Bollocks
Bullshit
Feck
Munter
Pissed/pissed off
Shit
Son of a bitch
Tits

Strong

Bastard
Beaver
Beef curtains
Bellend
Bloodclaat
Clunge
Cock
Dick
Dickhead
Fanny
Flaps
Gash
Knob
Minge
Prick
Punani
Pussy
Snatch
Twat

Strongest

Cunt
Fuck
Motherfucker

"YOU ARE WHAT YOU EAT, I'M A CUNT"

Bernard Manning

"TRY NOT TO BE A CUNT"

Buddha

Derivations

For such a strong word, cunt has surprisingly few derivations or associated sayings. Cunty, cuntish and cunted were only added into the *Oxford English Dictionary* in 2014.

	Usage	Meaning
Adjective	Cunty	To act like a cunt
Adjective	Cuntish	To act like a cunt
Verb	Cunted	To be drunk
Verb	Cunting	Intensify an insult

Chapter 8
{*Polite Swears*}

Polite Swears

Occasionally the circumstance may not allow a full swear. But there are plenty of alternatives that are safe for children's ears.

Oh fiddlesticks, I said fuck!

Root	Level 1	Level 2	Level 3
Fuck	Frick	Flip	Fiddlesticks
Shit	Crap	Shizzle	Sugar
Bollocks	Bollards	Balderdash	Blast
Dick	Cock	Knob	Pillock
Cunt	Twat	Twit	Twerp

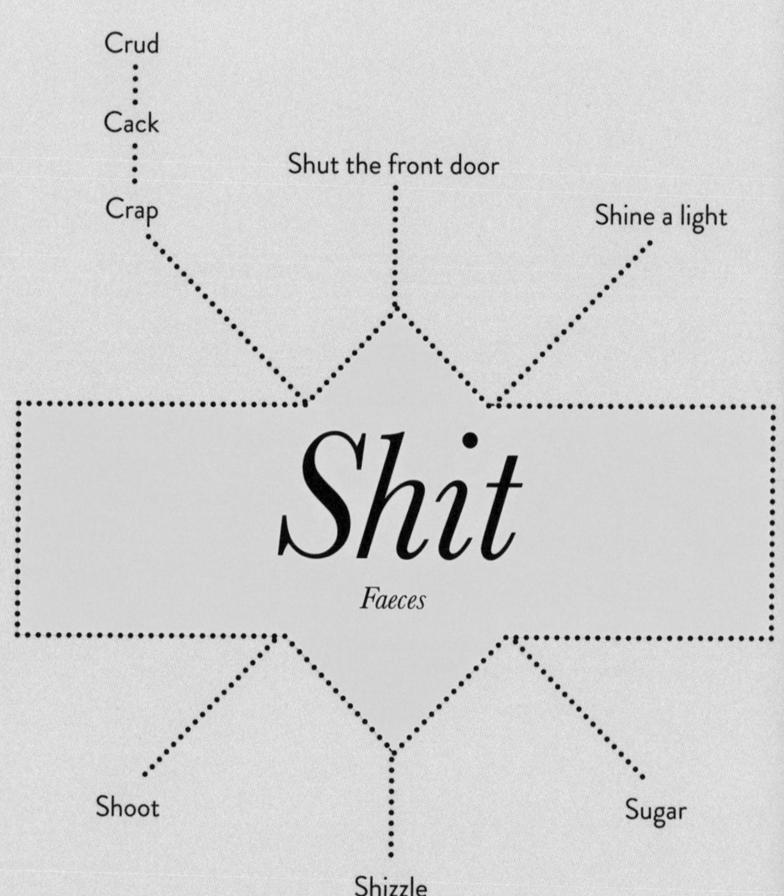
Crud
Cack
Crap
Shut the front door
Shine a light
Shit
Faeces
Shoot
Shizzle
Sugar

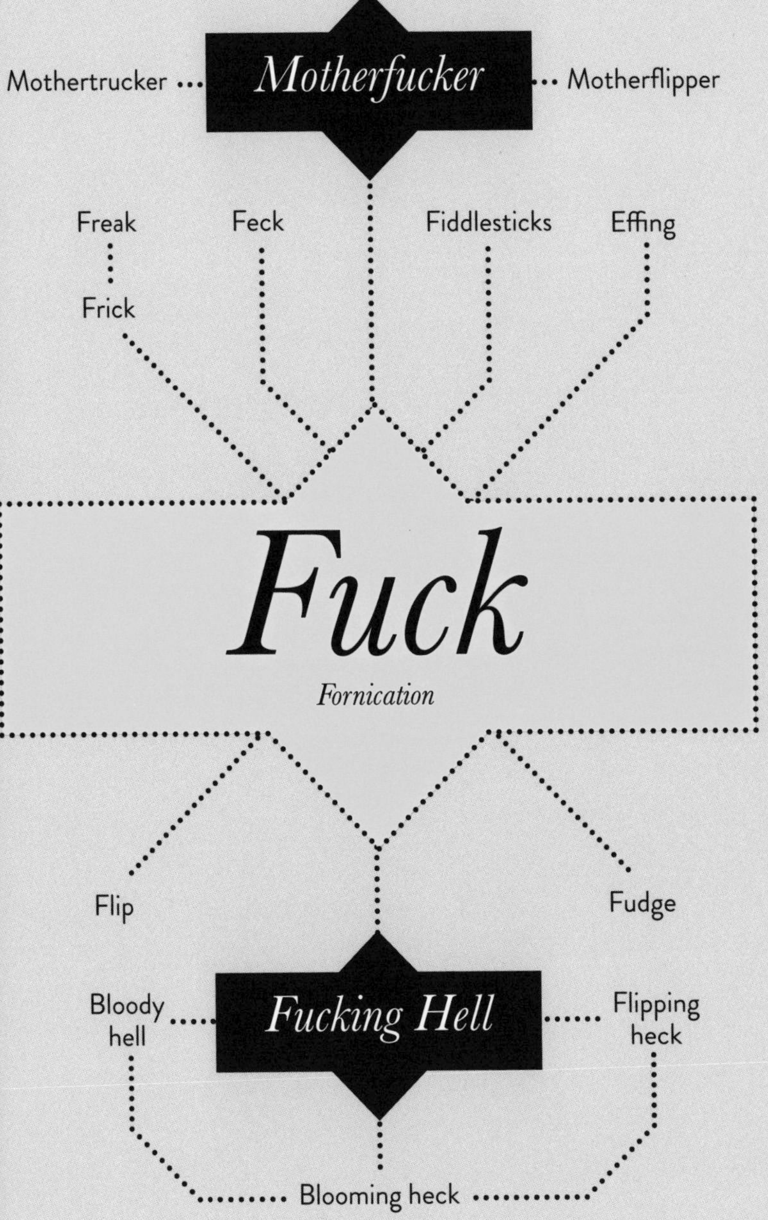
Mothertrucker
Motherfucker
Motherflipper
Freak
Frick
Feck
Fiddlesticks
Effing
Fuck
Fornication
Flip
Fudge
Bloody hell
Fucking Hell
Flipping heck
Blooming heck

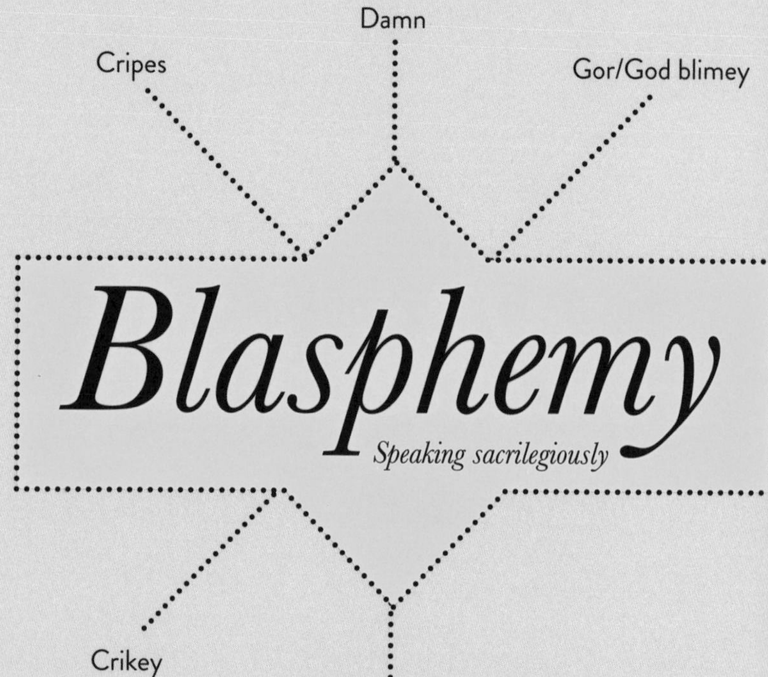
Damn
Cripes
Gor/God blimey
Blasphemy
Speaking sacrilegiously
Crikey
Jesus wept

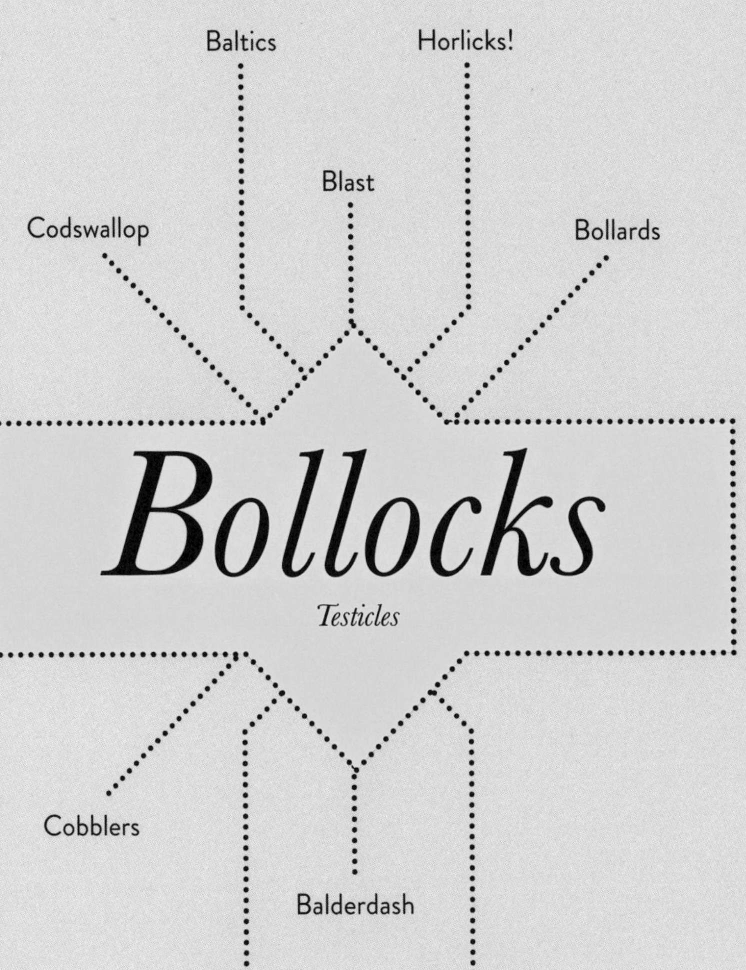
Baltics
Horlicks!
Blast
Codswallop
Bollards
Bollocks
Testicles
Cobblers
Balderdash
Ballcock
Rollocking

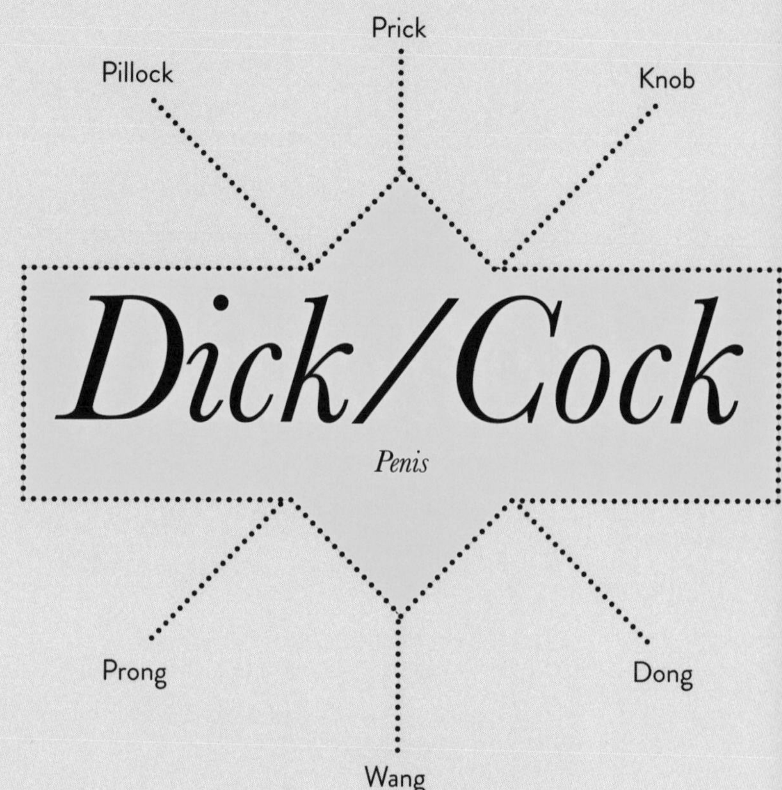
Prick
Pillock
Knob
Dick/Cock
Penis
Prong
Dong
Wang

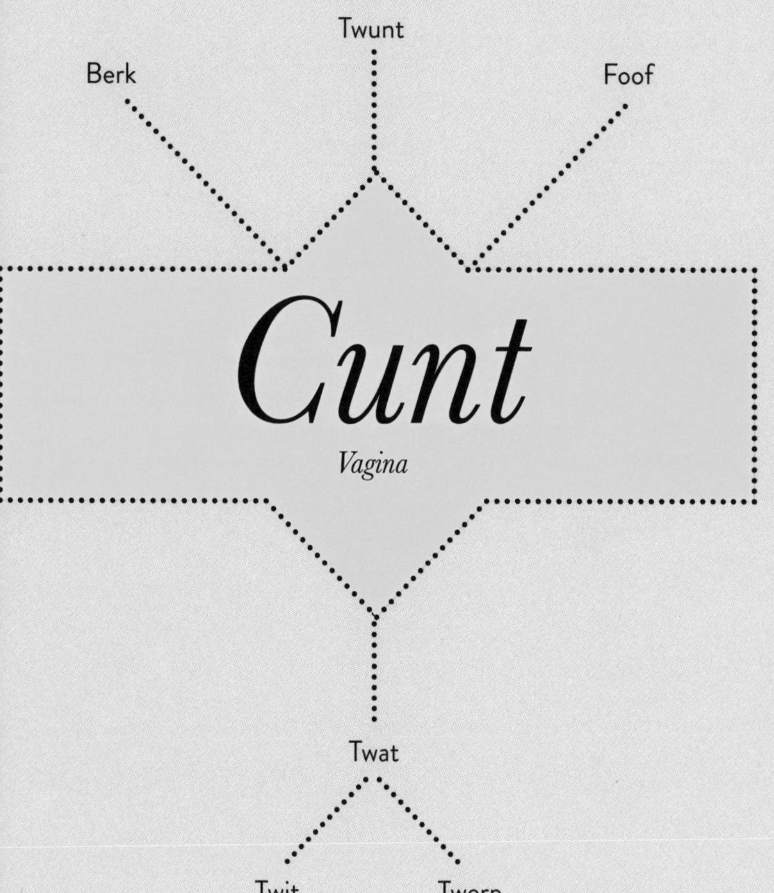
Twunt
Berk
Foof
Cunt
Vagina
Twat
Twit
Twerp

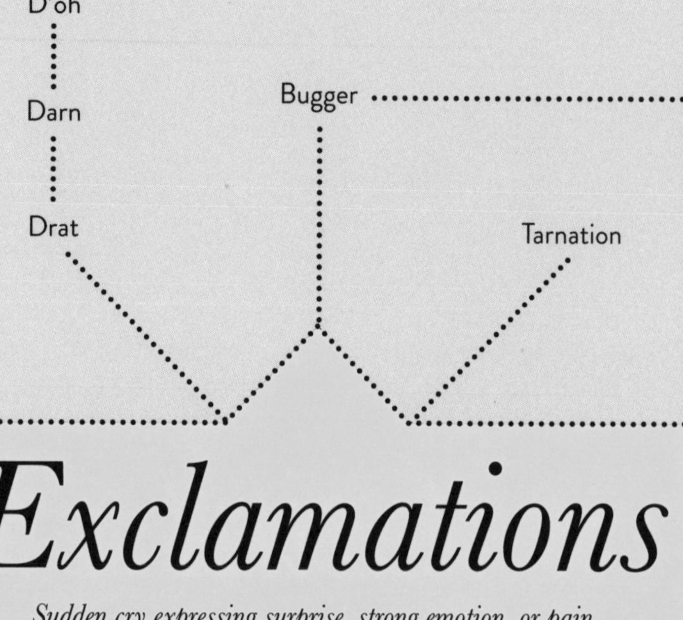

Exclamations

Sudden cry expressing surprise, strong emotion, or pain

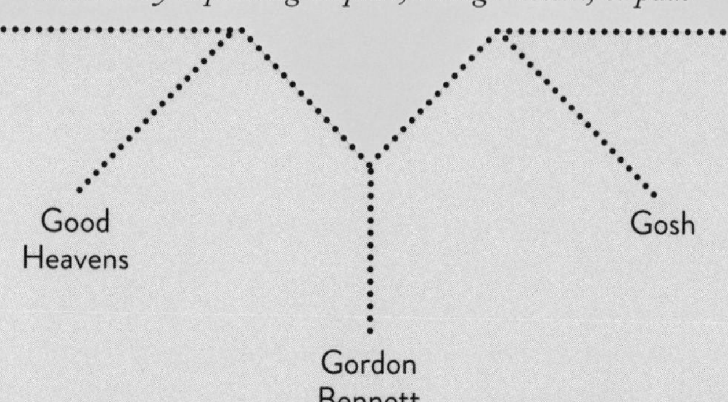

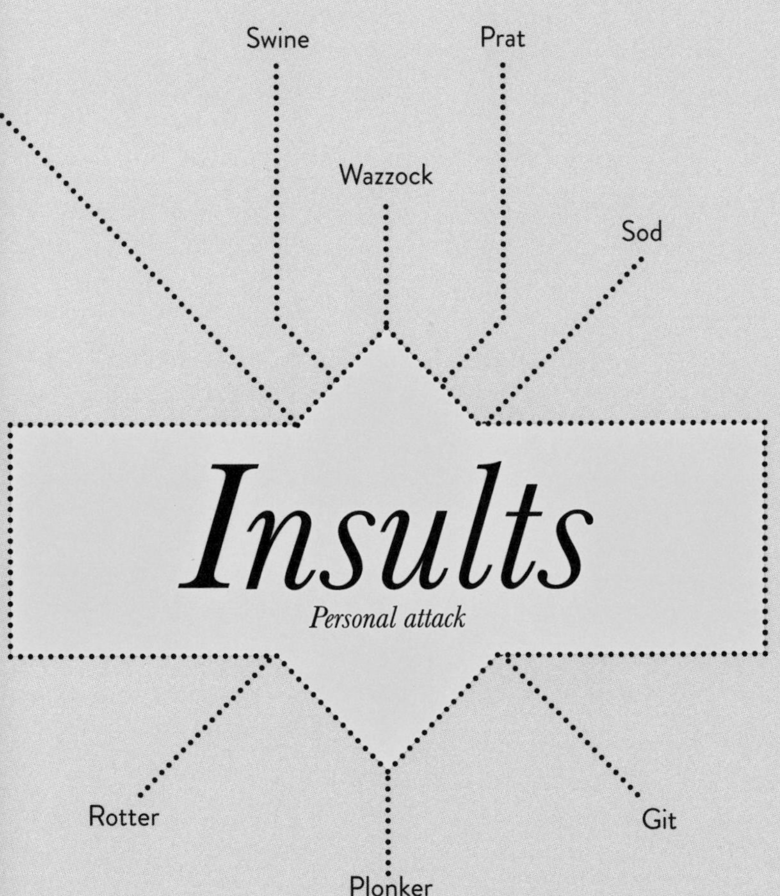
Swine
Prat
Wazzock
Sod
Insults
Personal attack
Rotter
Git
Plonker

Chapter 9
{*Hand Signals*}

Hand Signals

Obscene hand gestures are an ideal way to emphasise an insult. Or if a non-verbal insult is required (in traffic or over a large distance). Most hand gestures are sexually suggestive.

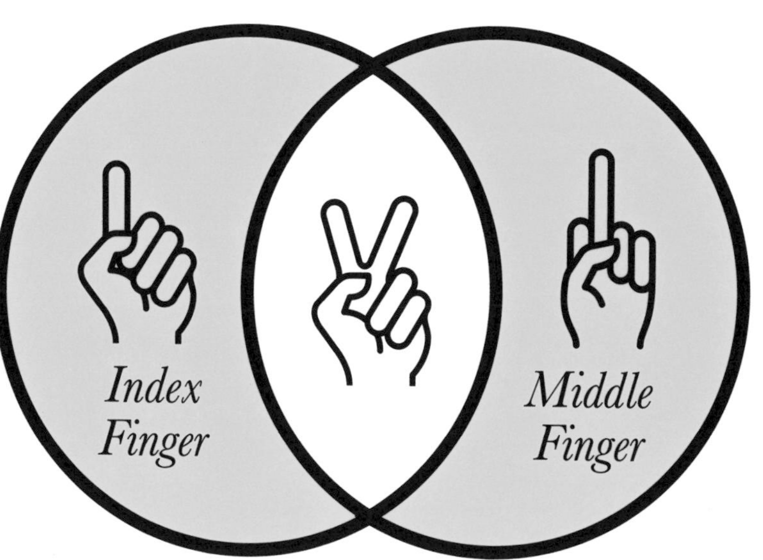
Index
Finger
Middle
Finger

Middle finger

To give someone the finger is equivalent to saying **fuck off**, **fuck you** or **up yours**.

It is performed by showing the back of a hand and raising the middle finger.

Showing the middle finger as an insult dates back to Ancient Greece. It represents the penis.

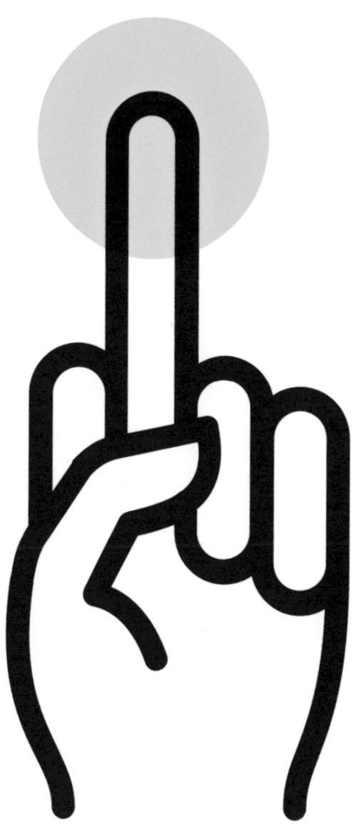

The bird

The finger

Flipping someone off

Two fingers

Showing two fingers is used to signify defiance (especially to authority).

To give a two-finger salute you place your hand with palm facing to you, raise the index and middle finger. Now raise your hand upwards from wrist with a flicking motion.

A common legend for the etymology of flicking the Vs is that it derives from a gesture made by English longbowmen fighting in the Battle of Agincourt. The legend states that captured bowmen had these two fingers removed so they could no longer fire their bows. Therefore, showing that you had these fingers was to demonstrate defiance. However good it sounds, there is no evidence for this origin.

Two-finger salute

Flicking the Vs

The forks

Wanker

Wanker is a term that means **one who wanks.** It is synonymous with the word tosser.

To perform the wanker signal you form your whole hand around an imaginary penis and move your hand from the wrist back and forth. For added effect you can shout "wanker".

One variation on the wanker hand signal is to move the fist to the forehead, where you mime masturbating an imaginary penis. With this hand signal you are calling the target a dickhead. The second is to perform the motion in front of your mouth, miming the act of fellatio.

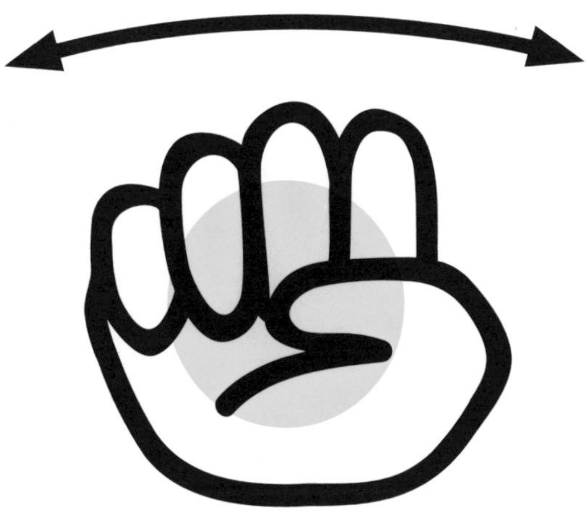

Wanker

Tosser

Dickhead
(performed on forehead)

Cocksucker
(perfomed in front of
an open mouth)

Appendix 1

A list of the most commonly used words.

Bottom

Anus
Arse
Arsehole
Arselicker
Arsewipe
Ass
Butt

Foolish

Clusterfuck
Dipshit
Douchebag
Dumbass
Fucktard
Fuckwit
Jackass

Derogatory

Bastard
Bint
Bitch
Son of a bitch
Slut
Thundercunt
Whore

Female Parts

Axewound
Beaver
Boobs
Camel toe
Clit
Clunge
Cunt
Fanny
Gash
Minge
Muff
Norks
Pissflaps
Punani
Pussy
Quim
Snatch
Tits
Tuppence
Twat
Vag

Sex Acts

Blow job
Bugger
Cocksucker
Fellatio
Feltch
Fuck
Fuckface
Handjob
Jerk off
Motherfucker
Tosser
Tosspot
Wanker

Blasphemy

Bloody
Damn
Goddamn
Jesus Christ

Male Parts

Balls
Bellend
Bollocks
Cock
Cockhead
Dick
Dickhead
Dickwad
Fuckstick
Knob
Nuts
Nutsack
Prick
Schlong

Excretions

Bullshit
Crap
Fart
Piss
Queef
Shart
Shat
Shit
Turd

Appendix 2

Getting it wrong

Breaking the rules when swearing can be interpreted as playful improvisation. To break the rules, use swearing not in common use or that defies any meaning or sense of the original words. Ironic use like this can show you know the rules and just don't care.

"Stick it up your bollocks,
you jizzcock"

Susan Wildish

Richard Pickles

Jake Allnutt

Simon Crotum

Jamie Stapleton

Suzanne Mathews

Walter Wildish